Christian Living
in the Mature Years

Vol. 53, No. 4   Summer 2021

Editorial/Design Team
Rachel Mullen, Acquisitions Editor
Rachel Hagewood, Editor of Bible Lessons
Keitha Vincent, Designer
Julie P. Glass, Production Editor

Administrative Staff
Rev. Brian K. Milford, President and Publisher
Marjorie M. Pon, Associate Publisher and Editor,
                Church School Publications

CHRISTIAN LIVING IN THE MATURE YEARS (ISSN 2639-8931)
is published quarterly by Abingdon Press, 2222 Rosa L. Parks Blvd.,
Nashville, TN 37228-1306. Periodicals Postage Paid at Nashville, TN, and
at additional mailing offices. POSTMASTER: Send address changes to
CHRISTIAN LIVING IN THE MATURE YEARS, 2222 Rosa L. Parks
Blvd., Nashville, TN 37228-1306.

Scripture quotations in this publication, unless otherwise noted, are from
the Common English Bible, copyright 2011. Used by permission. All rights
reserved.

For permission to reprint any material in this publication, call
615-749-6421, or write to Permissions Office, 2222 Rosa L. Parks Blvd.,
Nashville, TN 37228-1306.
Email: *permissions@abingdonpress.com.*

All Web addresses were correct and operational at the time of publication.

To order copies of this publication, call toll free: 800-672-1789. Use your
Cokesbury account, American Express, Visa, Discover, or Mastercard.

CHRISTIAN LIVING IN THE MATURE YEARS is designed to help
persons in and nearing the retirement years understand and appropriate
the resources of the Christian faith in dealing with specific problems and
opportunities related to aging.

Cover Photo: Shutterstock

Upload unsolicited manuscripts, photos, and cartoon submissions to
https://matureyears.submittable.com/submit in order to be considered for use.

Christian Living
in the Mature Years

19

28

34

35

The Friendship Initiative
by Amberly Neese

If there ever was a time we needed true connection with others—to cultivate meaningful relationships—this is it. *The Friendship Initiative,* a 31-day devotional by Amberly Neese, is a great place to start. Not only will you find encouragement and practical help for connecting with others, you'll learn how to do so following Jesus' example. You'll discover thirty-one new keys for building relationships every day, like exercising grace, having compassion, and being present. Each daily reading includes Scripture, a reflection, practical application ideas, and suggestions for prayer that focus on loving others as Jesus did.

Courage: Jesus and the Call to Brave Faith
by Tom Berlin

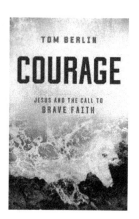

As Christians, we do our best to live our lives as Jesus lived, following the examples of his many virtues—including honesty, faithfulness, and generosity. But one virtue that is often overlooked is courage. Throughout Jesus' life, he was called upon to be brave: in the face of his enemies, when being tempted, and certainly at the time of his death. By examining the life of Christ, we can begin to understand what true courage is and how God works in our lives when we exhibit a brave faith. Pastor and author Tom Berlin challenges us to unlock the courage that we already possess as Christ followers, and in doing so, we can begin to find the remarkable life Jesus offers us.

Come Back
by Roger Ross

Divorce, betrayal, health issues, financial woes . . . many of life's situations make us wish we could go back and have a do-over. Of course, turning back the clock is not an option, but transforming or renewing our lives, even if it feels too late, is a definite choice. It's not too late. In fact, you were made for a turnaround. You don't need a spiritual pedigree to start the journey, just a heartfelt desire to see your life change and openness to the process. That's it. The rest will be revealed along the way.

Looking for God in Messy Places
by Jake Owensby

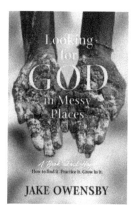

Hope is the power that gets us out of bed in morning and gives us the courage to face adversity. But often we lose hope in busyness, comparison—the messy places of life. *Looking for God in Messy Places* by Jake Owensby is a book about hope. How to find it. How to practice it. How to grow in it. How it makes life worth living. Because when we look for God in the middle of the mess, we find hope.

This book is for anyone who has ever been frozen in place by loss or regret; anyone who has endured suffering, cruelty, or rejection. From word to word and page to page, readers will experience themselves as God's beloved—so that they can be hopeful.

The Wesley Prayer Challenge
by Chris Folmsbee

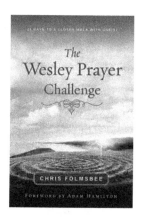

The Wesley Covenant Prayer has been used in Methodist services around the world on the first Sunday of the year since John Wesley introduced it in 1755. Wesley expected that people would pray this prayer as a way of remembering, renewing, and surrendering themselves in complete trust to God. In *The Wesley Prayer Challenge,* author Chris Folmsbee invites readers to consider words from the Wesley Covenant Prayer each day for three weeks, while reflecting on their meaning in the context of the larger piece. A Scripture, a prayer, and a challenge for daily life are also included each day.

Read sample chapters and find more information at
AbingdonPress.com

On Water Skis

BY ROBERT H. SPAIN

Recently, I watched on TV an exhibition by water-skiers. They were magnificent. It was far more than an athletic event. It was a fabulous display of artistic expression. They did on water what some display upon a canvas. Two skiers being pulled along by a high-powered engine danced their way in, out, and through the wake from the boat. They did amazing twists and turns over, around, and through the waves. They were gliding on the water as Olympic ice-skaters would magically capture the ice. They moved with the grace and precision of the high-wire trapeze artist or the ballerina with elegance and poise seamlessly floating across the stage.

I was reminded of my introduction to waterskiing. It was a long time ago—more than sixty years. For most of us in Overton County, it was a new water adventure that had to be experienced. Keep in mind this was in the days before fancy designed skis and big 100-horsepower engines. Our skis were handmade, and the aluminum fishing boat was powered with two 10-horsepower motors jerry-rigged to the back of the boat. The anticipated day finally arrived. My teacher was a skinny twelve-year-old. He began the lesson by first showing me how it is done. He did it well. He positioned himself in the water, the boat jerked him into a gliding position, and off he went. Nothing to it. My turn. Being the practical person I am, I carefully followed the instructions. I positioned myself in the water, leaned back with my hands firmly holding the rope—the tip of the skis pointing up and out of the water—and yelled to the driver. It was horrible. The boat lunged, the tips of the skis went down instead of up, and that boat dragged me headfirst halfway across Dale Hollow Lake.

The old adage is that practice makes perfect. I practiced a lot and it indeed became rewarding, but it took a little help and a lot of ups and downs.

In some ways, my Christian pilgrimage has mimicked some of my waterskiing. It wasn't a once-and-done quest. The journey in our relationship with the Lord takes different paths. Some are knocked down with lightning bolts and radically transported into a new life. The apostle Paul apparently had something like this happen to him. But with others, our paths are longer and often filled with unwanted detours. I have often thought about getting everything with the Lord firmly fixed and carefully wrapped and tied with a neat bow, but it doesn't happen. I doubt that it ever will, but with the Lord at my side, the journey is still exciting.

Robert H. Spain is a retired United Methodist bishop and former chaplain of The United Methodist Publishing House.

My Sister and the Chickens

BY MARION TURNBULL

My sister came home with a big cardboard box in her arms and a huge smile on her face. She put the box down.

"You know that horrible chicken farm down the road?"

I knew it, and we used to shudder when we passed the "egg-producing factory," where rows of poor hens were tucked into small cages. All they could do was stick out a head to feed, and their eggs dropped onto a conveyor belt. No sun allowed—electric lights controlled their day and night. You could smell the stench and misery.

"I was passing the farm today," my sister announced, "and they were selling off older hens. They pushed twelve of the poor things into a box, so I bought one."

"What are we going to do with them?"

"You know that old henhouse in the yard with a wire chicken run? I'm going to fix it. At least I can give these a bit of a life," she announced as she swept out the henhouse and mended the wire fence around the run.

The box was carried into the clean house. "There you are," she whispered as she put them carefully, one by one, onto the floor. "Look! You can walk about, sit in the boxes to lay your eggs, or go outside into the sun through that tiny, little door. Come on now!"

The hens sat exactly where she had put them.

We scattered corn on the floor, and they stuck out their necks to grab it and to drink from a dish, but they shrank back into a huddle. Of course! They had never been free, and the poor things didn't know what to do.

The next day, they were still sitting together on the floor. "Move around and go into the sunshine," she told them. But the hens stayed put, even when we picked up some eggs from their feet.

At last, after three days, one brave hen stuck its neck out of the doorway. It put one foot slowly in front of the other until it was outside—then jumped back in again. The next day, it was outside and scratching around, as free hens do. Another hen joined it. It took two more days before the others followed, but once they got the idea, it was wonderful to see them pecking up the corn we threw, scratching around in the sunshine, and clucking happily away.

My sister was delighted. She was able to collect some eggs from those hens—not always laid in the proper places, but fresh every morning—and the hens were free at last.

"Just like people," she said. "Jesus came to set us free, but some of us don't realize it—yet."

Free from what? The hens had never experienced the sun or freedom to move about, so they were slow to find out. It's the same with us. We get all penned up in our little lives and can miss out on all the gifts and opportunities God puts in front of our noses because we don't really believe they are for us. But God is open to all of us through Jesus. Nothing can stop us stepping out and breathing in the fresh air of heaven. Nothing at all.

"The law of the Spirit of life in Christ Jesus has set you free from the law of sin and death" (Romans 8:2).

So, let's step out and explore everything God wants to give us.

Slow TV

You may have heard of the Slow Movement, which advocates a shift to a slower, more conscious pace of life. A popular component of this is the Slow Food Movement, which encourages people to forgo fast food for traditional cooking. I personally love the idea of the Slow Movement. I'm incredibly busy most of the time (aren't we all?), and consciously stepping out of the rushing river of life to enjoy a home-cooked meal or spend time with my family feels so refreshing.

I was browsing through my television streaming service's documentary offerings a few weeks ago when I stumbled across a series called "Slow TV." Apparently, while we've been focusing on television programs that are BIGGER, FASTER, MORE here in the United States, in Norway the opposite has been happening. A wildly popular series called "Slow TV" broadcasts events, such as a seven-hour train ride or someone knitting for four hours in real time. There are no plots, no characters, no car chases or explosions.

Intrigued and a little skeptical, I started the first episode, "Train Ride: Bergen to Oslo." A camera mounted on the front of the train broadcast the entire journey, winding through the mountains of Norway. The view darkened in tunnels, announcements were made, people mumbled in the background at station stops. Other than that, nothing happened. Nothing. I thought I would watch a few minutes, then scoff while returning to my action-packed queue.

But I was mesmerized. I watched the train for more than an hour. It felt a lot like meditating, letting my mind focus not on a storyline, but on changing scenery, falling rain, and whooshing wind. I fell into the rhythm of the *ca-chunk-ca-chunk* of the train on the tracks, and I loved every drawn-out minute of it!

As much as anyone, I need to learn to slow down in my everyday life. I need to take time to focus on my family, to enjoy a meal without worrying about where I need to be next. I need to pray without simply running down a list of "thank yous" and "I wants." I need to take the time to enjoy the gifts I have been given, and also to feel the grief and pain I carry with me. All of this is part of God's amazing creation, and I owe it to God and to myself to experience it fully, consciously . . . slowly.

My Violin

BY PABLO GARZON

When my father died from a sudden heart attack, I was thirteen years old. To help us deal with our grief, my mother enrolled my sister and me in a music academy. The teacher was a violinist who taught the class by playing his violin. I had never been near a violin before. Since the moment I first saw it and heard it in that class, I was completely in love with the violin.

I studied with that teacher for two years. After that, I took private classes at the Conservatory. Then I stopped playing the violin to study philosophy at Los Andes University in Bogotá. I traveled to Nashville with a Fulbright Scholarship to attend Vanderbilt University. After I graduated, I returned to Bogotá only to come back to Nashville to work at United Methodist Communications.

The same year, some friends invited me to spend Christmas and New Year's with them in Huntsville, Alabama. My friends happened to have a violin. They encouraged me to play, and they allowed me to take that violin home with me to Nashville, with the condition that I start taking lessons. I obediently obliged.

The violin my friends lent me belonged to an elderly man who fought in Germany during the Second World War. He found the instrument broken in the street of a German city, brought it back to the USA, and fixed it.

After many years without playing at all, I took violin lessons for adults. I have been playing regularly since. I now have my own violin, and I formed a band to play Latin American music.

Thanks to my jobs with United Methodist agencies, I have used the violin in my ministry. I learned and played beautiful hymns from *The UM Hymnal*. This, in turn, has allowed me to play for chapel services and different events. In 2018, I had the great honor to play one of the Violins of Hope for an event at a local synagogue. Violins of Hope is a collection of violins that were found in concentration camps and belonged to Jewish musicians.

I can see how God has led me to music to grow spiritually and reach others. Even though I became serious about playing late in life, I have found great satisfaction and meaning in the strings of my violin.

How to Handle a
Bee Sting

BY RHONDA DELPH

How do you envision your journey through life? Do you see life as strolling through a field of flowers? (Is it roses or daisies?) Is it like a box of chocolates? Or is life your battlefield, as you trudge through a course of hidden, explosive mines? While it would be easy to see a challenge-filled life as a battlefield, I try to embrace it as a field of clover.

As a child, a yard full of clover was a playground. The carpeted ground provided a soft place for a kid to sprawl for games, relaxation, and cloud-watching, or simply to explore the lush evergreen plant. I would gather a bouquet of the usually white-topped blooms, or tie stems together to create necklace strands. But more importantly, the typically tri-foil greenery created camouflage for the "lucky" four-leaf clover! Even at 65, I still find myself hesitating when I pass a patch of clover, head down, trying to spot that elusive, smile-producing prize of four leaves.

But often in fields of clover, one can come across an occasional bee, doing its job, collecting nectar. I avoided bees in fear of being stung, but stings did happen. In the case of a sting, I tried to accept the surprise of the sting and the subsequent pain, then run to my mother for her comfort and support.

As an adult trekking through life's field of clover, I may give the appearance that I'm enjoying a casual stroll through life while hopscotching through the little ups and downs. But in reality, I know that a big scary bee sting could appear at any time. When those stings do inevitably happen, I reach out to the Lord. God holds me close, providing comfort, strength, and healing, even when the lingering pain of some stings compels me to never leave God's side and loving presence.

With every sting of life, I learn that God's direction and comfort help me manage the pain. I know that God is there to dry my tears and prepare me to return to the clover fields given to me to enjoy and share with others.

Life is a precious gift from God. I am here to glorify God and praise God! How I am affected in my journey through the clover fields makes me who I am. I can enjoy the carpeted expanses of blessings, while also being an example of God's loving provision and care when I'm stung.

So, bring it on, bees! I know the One who soothes the pain!

Leap Years and Bucket Lists

BY LORI HATCHER

February 29, 2020, Leap Year Day, seemed like a great day to do something unusual. Twenty-three friends and I were on a cruise ship sailing toward the Bahamas, celebrating the end of our journey as home educators. My options for unusual were as broad as my imagination.

Eat something scary from the *Things You've Always Wanted to Try* list in the ship's dining room? Nah. Choking down braised ox tongue was a little too unusual for my taste.

Get a hot rocks massage in the spa? I've never had one, so that would be different, but the $129.00 price tag scared me away.

Gamble in the casino? Nope. Money is too hard to come by, and I'm not about to risk it on a spin of the wheel.

That left one option: **the high ropes course.**

Suspended 150 feet above the deck of the ship, the 230-foot spiderweb of ropes, bridges, swinging steps, and balance beams provided the perfect opportunity to do something I'd never done before. And the best view on the ship—if I didn't pass out from fright.

From what I'd read, the most challenging time to tackle the course is on a sea day. The movement of the ship combined with sometimes gusty winds make navigating the ropes course even more difficult.

February 29 just happened to be a sea day.

But completing a high ropes course had always been on my bucket list, so I queued up.

The guide instructed me to climb into a canvas harness attached to a tether anchored to a metal cable five feet above the ropes course. She crisscrossed straps over my shoulders, clicked a few carabiners, and cinched everything tight. My friend Maryann lined up behind me.

"What if I don't like it?" she said, looking down at the deck below.

"Then you keep moving," the guide said. "There's no turning back."

Feeling like a contestant on a television show, I faced the first challenge—a footbridge comprised of twelve-inch wooden steps held together with rope and swaying in the wind.

"Don't look down. Don't look at the other climbers. Just focus on the next step," the guide said as I hesitated at the edge of the platform. Why did I think this was a good idea?

But the only way out was through, so I stepped off the platform and onto the first step. Gripping the one-inch ropes on either side of the bridge, I made my way across one trembling step at a time.

Step. Wobble wobble. Step. Sway sway. Step. Step. Step. Step. Step. Wobble sway, wobble sway. Wobble.

And then the big step that brought me onto the next stable pedestal. Hallelujah! One part of the journey complete.

I took a few deep breaths to ensure I didn't pass out, then considered the next challenge. As much as I wanted to hang out on the blissfully-stable platform, I couldn't linger. There were people behind me.

Ahead of me stretched a net of ropes crisscrossing like a tic-tac-toe grid. One misstep and my foot would slip through a square, trapping me like a fly in a spider's web.

Behind me, my friend Maryann was struggling. Her legs are shorter than mine and her fear of heights greater. She was in trouble.

"Don't look down!" one friend called from below.

"You can do this!" another said from behind her.

"One step at a time," yelled another, her camera poised to capture every moment.

I called instructions from ahead. "Put your feet in the center of the boards. Only four more to go. You're almost there."

A few more wobbly steps, and she was close enough for me to reach out and boost her onto the platform. She smiled weakly and laid her hand on her heart. "Why did I ever agree to this?"

But the only way out was through, so we set off. I went first to find the footholds, while those behind us cheered us on.

Finally, we reached the most difficult portion of the course—two thin ropes beneath our feet with nothing to hold on to except the tether strap that anchored us to the cable above our heads.

"Hold on to the strap," the guide yelled. "Trust the anchor. It's got you."

There, dangling between heaven and earth, I saw my life as God sees it.

We leave the safe cocoon of our mothers and step onto the path ordained for us. We can't see

the destination, only the path ahead. The only way out is through.

Yet, God doesn't send us out alone.

If we've placed our faith in God, God sets the course before us. God hems us in behind and before. God surrounds us with caring people—parents, siblings, and brothers and sisters in Christ—to show us the way.

Those who have navigated similar obstacles share their wisdom and encouragement. Others warn us away from danger and slippery paths. Fellow travelers facing the same challenges inspire us with their companionship and love. Friends reach out to lift us up.

And if that isn't enough, higher than the highest ropes course stands a great cloud of witnesses cheering us on (Hebrews 12:1).

And when we reach the most difficult part of our journey, the places we have to walk alone? It's then that we discover we're not alone after all. Jesus is there.

We hold tightly to the Anchor, knowing that if we stumble, slip, or lose our grip, the Lord will hold us fast. God promises to never let us go (Deuteronomy 31:8).

God will bring us safely to the other side.

Where are you in your faith journey?

Have you taken your first trembling steps? Seek out brothers and sisters in Christ to walk with you.

Have you navigated trials and grown stronger because of them? Look around for someone who can benefit from your wisdom and experience.

Are you in the hardest place? Surround yourself with God's people and cling to Jesus. Rest in the secure knowledge that God is holding on to you and will never ever let you go.

God will see you safely through.

Lori Hatcher is the author of Refresh Your Faith, Uncommon Devotions from Every Book of the Bible. *She and her pastor/husband live delightfully close to their four grandchildren in Lexington, South Carolina. Read her five-minute devotions at* www.LoriHatcher.com.

This Is Important

BY JAN TURRENTINE

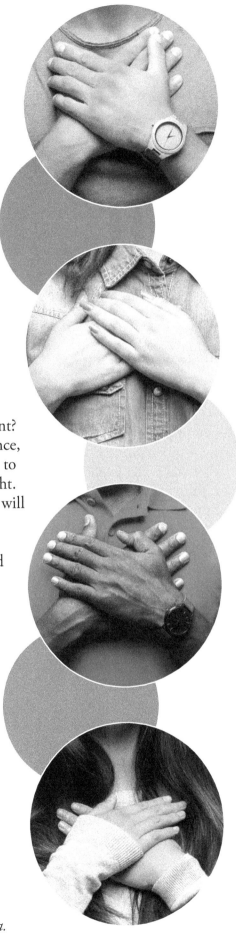

And every day," author Iain S. Thomas wrote, "the world will drag you by the hand, yelling, 'This is important! And this is important! And this is important! You need to worry about this! And this! And this!' And each day, it's up to you to yank your hand back, put it on your heart and say, 'No. This is what's important'" *(https://iainsthomas.com/about/).*

A brilliant piece of writing, this paragraph moves from strident urgency to gentle determination. The cadence of the opening words pulls us along at an alarming speed; then the slow rhythm of the last line stops us suddenly in our tracks.

When you yank your hand away from the world's tight grasp and place it on your heart, what do you declare is most important? It's a question we must ask as followers of Christ, and ask not once, but every day. Because as Thomas said, every day the world tries to set our priorities for us. And every day, we must reclaim that right. We must decide each day that our thoughts, words, and actions will reflect the presence of Christ in our lives.

It's rarely an easy choice. That's why Jesus told would-be followers to count the cost. If we want easy, Jesus said, the world has plenty to offer. But none of it compares to the life we find in him. Our commitment to Christ must be more important than anything else. It must be our highest priority. When it is, we begin to develop the proper perspective on ourselves, others, and things. We learn to let go of the past, of our guilt, of things that weigh us down. And we learn to cling tightly to Christ, whose presence and power enable us to declare, "No. This is what's important." And with that declaration, with that power and presence in our lives, we can move courageously onto a path we may not understand and into a future we cannot predict.

What is most important to you?

"Those who find their lives will lose them," Jesus said, "and those who lose their lives because of me will find them" (Matthew 10:39).

Jan Turrentine is lead editor for adult resources with Cokesbury. She has written and edited a number of books and Christian education curricula.

Adventures in Self-isolating

BY DAPHNA FLEGAL AND DEB SMITH

The spring of 2020 brought a surprising event: coronavirus. I was looking forward to spring. I planned a trip to a national quilt festival in a nearby city; I had tickets to see the band Chicago; and I was attending my great-nephew's high school graduation. Suddenly, all of that was gone. Events were canceled, and we were told to stay home—to isolate ourselves from our friends, families, and neighbors. No eating out, no getting haircuts, and no graduations. While I grieved the loss of "normalcy," I quickly realized I could either watch the news twenty-four hours a day or find new adventures. I chose adventure.

One of the first things I did was spend more time on my favorite hobby: quilting. I began with a baby quilt for my friend's baby due in May. I had stacks of UFOs (unfinished objects) just waiting for my attention. It was satisfying to spend time on a hobby without guilt. There really wasn't anything else I should be doing.

I have a friend whose hobby is photography. What began as taking photos of birds from her deck led her to want to learn more about the lives of these feathered neighbors. While many serious bird-watchers have life lists of all the birds they have seen, she now has an isolation list. The experience was enriched by an online subscription to a comprehensive ornithology resource and an app to help her identify new birds.

I was not allowed to visit my granddaughter for fourteen days. But after fourteen days with no symptoms within my family, I started keeping my granddaughter three days a week. Her parents both worked from home, and her visits with me gave everyone a break. We spent mornings with her homework and afternoons baking cookies, baking cakes, and of course, making slime.

Technology and media became very important to me. I even learned some new things, like how to video conference with Zoom. The monthly lunch group I met with became a monthly Zoom meeting, with some of us wearing hats to cover our unstyled hair. I FaceTimed with my daughter frequently and I called my sister, who lives out of town, every morning. I looked at YouTube videos to learn new techniques for quilting. I even signed up for a free online class that a university was offering. And thanks to modern technology, I could check out and read books online from the library.

Fred Rogers is reported as saying that when something bad happens, you need to look for the helpers. Certainly, we saw lots and lots of helpers during the pandemic: doctors, nurses, EMTs, first-responders, police, and many more. These helpers were asking for face masks, so I became a helper and sewed many masks that I gave to nurses and firefighters. I also offered face masks

to family and friends who did not sew. It felt good to be a helper.

My friend with the photography hobby also became a mask-maker. She discovered a way to transfer her photographs to fabric and started making masks with photos on them. Reclaiming and adapting a childhood tradition of leaving May baskets on friends' doorsteps, she delivered homemade drawstring bags filled with candy and masks on May Day. It gave her great pleasure to select photos that would be meaningful to the person receiving the mask, and it brightened the day of those receiving the masks.

Church became even more important. Sunday services were posted online, and we held Sunday school through Zoom. I even found myself visiting other churches, sometimes in other states, through their online services. It was easier to participate in church committee meetings, since I didn't have to drive anywhere. Our Creation Care team sponsored a virtual Earth Day celebration, with videos and photos to encourage environmental stewardship.

I started walking every day. My walks got me out of the house and into springtime. I could see flowers bud and bloom. I watched as birds built nests. Normally, exercise is something I'm going to get around to, not actually do. I discovered I enjoyed the time walking in nature.

I cooked. This was really out of my norm. I'm more likely to pick up takeout or a packaged meal rather than make one. I started eating more healthy meals. I rediscovered favorite recipes I'd made when my children were young, and I tried out new ones. I kept an ongoing grocery list to make sure my monthly grocery trips included needed items for my culinary adventures. Instead of eating my meals on the couch while watching TV, I set the table with my best china, place mats, and cloth napkins. I made meals for my friend after her baby was born and left them on her doorstep.

As I write this article, I have no idea how or when the pandemic will end. I do know that even though I was isolated, I was in contact with friends and family. I had meaningful work to do and new adventures to discover. I kept my mind and body engaged. These lessons I learned will serve me well long after this pandemic has ended.

Daphna Flegal is retired from The United Methodist Publishing House, where she served for twenty-five years as Lead Editor in the Children's Department. She enjoys reading, quilting, traveling, and being with her granddaughter.

Deb Smith is a retired deacon in the Tennessee Conference of The United Methodist Church. She enjoys reading, photography, and advocating for healthcare and creation care.

On Looking Up

BY BRIAN SIGMON

Y

ou only see shooting stars if you're looking up.

The first time I saw one, I was in high school. My dad and I were going up to the mountains one Saturday for a bricklaying job, and we'd gathered with a bunch of others in a parking lot to drive up together. It was early morning—clear, still dark—but the sky in the east was getting lighter. We stood around outside our trucks, chatting and looking around like men used to do before we all got phones to shove our noses into. Somebody said, "Wow!" and pointed overhead. I happened to turn and look up fast enough to see the meteor still streaking across the sky before it blinked out. I don't remember much about that bricklaying job, but two decades later, I still recall the feeling of exhilaration at seeing something rare and beautiful because somebody had been paying attention.

Paying attention has always been a holy act, though it's now a lost art. Maybe it always has been. Turning our attention and focus outward removes ourselves from the center of our world, often a necessary condition for encountering God. We need reminding that our desires, grievances, obstacles, worries, and pleasures are not as important as they usually feel. Looking up, paying attention to something else, helps me understand that the world is wide and most of it is not me. And when we don't look up, we miss the opportunities afforded us by a larger perspective.

Moses paid attention. He heard God's call in the wilderness and boldly confronted Pharaoh. He led the Israelites out of slavery and through the Red Sea, taking them to meet God on the mountain and eventually shepherding them to the Promised Land. But it's easy to miss that Moses' first act was simply paying attention.

Moses saw that the bush was in flames, but it didn't burn up. Then Moses said to himself, Let me check out this amazing sight and find out why the bush isn't burning up. When the LORD saw that he was coming to look, God called to him out of the bush, "Moses, Moses!" (Exodus 3:2-4)

Moses' first step was to notice. He saw something out of place, asked a question about it, and went in for closer inspection. Only when God saw that Moses turned aside to see did God call to him with the commission that would change Moses' life.

I wonder if other shepherds passed by the burning bush without turning aside to see because they were too busy accounting for their herd. Perhaps Moses himself had walked past the site a few days in a row without really noticing the bush that burned but was never consumed. Or maybe not. Maybe Moses was in the habit of paying attention, looking at the mountain every day, so he knew right away when something on it was out of the ordinary. Whether it was momentary or habitual, Moses' act of paying attention, turning his focus outward and upward, was the act that opened the way for God to speak. It brought to him an opportunity to deliver his people and take his place in God's story of salvation.

You only see shooting stars if you're looking up.

Looking up is something I've been trying to do more of lately. It's a habit I'm striving to cultivate, and it's been deeply rewarding. My wife bought me a pair of binoculars for Christmas, and I've enjoyed using them to see the night sky in more detail. Ever since, I have found myself venturing outside every time the sky is clear at night. I've even gotten into the habit of going onto the deck in the early morning, before everyone else is awake, to stargaze a bit before my daily prayer and Scripture reading.

The practice has nurtured my wonder at the universe, my appreciation for just how mind-bogglingly vast and intricate our creation is. But all that was to be expected. What I didn't expect was how much I'd start to notice just because I was looking up more frequently.

I began to understand how the night sky changes in predictable ways over the course of an evening and in other predictable ways over the course of several months. I noticed that Orion was lower in the sky if I went out earlier, and higher if I went out later. I saw how Orion and Taurus moved gradually from east to west as the

> *[W]hen we don't look up, we miss the opportunities afforded us by a larger perspective.*

months progressed. I saw how the Big Dipper rotates around the northern sky, but remains visible both in the evening and in the morning. I saw the Moon on one side of Jupiter one morning, and then on the other side of Jupiter the next morning. Using the binoculars, I've even seen some of Jupiter's moons and noticed how they move from one morning to the next, but still stay near Jupiter. I've watched Sagittarius recently become visible in the southern sky in the predawn hour, and I know that it will gradually rise earlier and earlier.

None of this is new information, of course. Astronomers have watched and charted these movements in the sky for thousands of years. The slow movement of the stars has always been there to be noticed by those who look up, pay attention, and seek to understand. What's changed is my own attentiveness, my consistency in looking up, and a more robust framework for understanding what I see.

Doing so has broadened my perspective. It's easier to remember that the ground beneath us spins through 360 degrees of rotation once a day when you see the stars gradually change positions as the hour gets later. It's easier to recall that our planet hurdles through space at 67,000 miles per hour when you see evidence of it in the night sky as the months pass. The world's problems, my problems, suddenly become smaller when I consider them within this cosmic perspective. And at the same time, my impression of God becomes far larger when I realize that even these vast distances and speeds are as nothing to the Creator.

Paying attention also shifts my experience of time, attuning it a bit more with nature's rhythms rather than measuring it solely by my watch and alarm clock. I know that, soon, I'll no longer be able to see Orion at night, and the next time it becomes visible I'll be thinking about Christmas. I know that the next time Sagittarius sits low in the southern sky at 5:00 a.m., I'll have seen twelve more full moons and I'll be a year older. Paying attention sets my problems and my joys in perspective, and helps me see how precious time is on this earth. It's important to look up.

One morning a few weeks ago, I stood on my back deck with my binoculars. I was looking up through the bare branches of the trees beside my house, trying to find the North Star. But before it came into view, I saw a streak of light through my binocular lens. It flashed for a moment right through my field of vision, and then it was gone. It was too fast to have been an airplane and too small to have been an animal up in the tree branches. I knew it was a shooting star, streaking for a brief instant then winking out. I said, "Oh, wow!" and offered a silent prayer of thanks to God for allowing me to see something extraordinary on a routine weekday morning.

I was very lucky that I happened to have my binoculars on that narrow patch of sky at just the right moment, so that I glimpsed the meteor when it passed.

You only see shooting stars if you're looking up.

Do you find, like I do, that you wish you looked up more? What do you need to turn your attention away from? How can paying attention to your surroundings, whether it's the night sky or the changing seasons or the people around you, give you a better perspective on your life? What opportunities might there be for you if you take the time to look upward and outward?

Brian O. Sigmon is editor of United Methodist resources at The United Methodist Publishing House. Brian has a PhD in Old Testament Studies from Marquette University, where he also taught courses in theology. He also has a deep love of physics and space exploration, and he blogs about the intersection of faith and space at starstruckchristian.wordpress.com. *Brian finds great joy in helping people of all backgrounds deepen their understanding of Scripture.*

What Does God Look Like?

BY KATIE SHOCKLEY

I read an article online about an illustrator who talked with a group of children about what they imagine God looks like. The children gave varied, and often humorous, descriptions of God's physical appearance, and the illustrator drew what they described, asking them questions along the way for clarity. One child said that God has a frog's body with a lion's head. Another child said God wears a Mohawk haircut, while another child said God has wings with attached hands which hold a hot dog, in case God gets hungry.

God is beyond human comprehension. No human language has words precise enough to describe God or God's physical form. Hence, even if we could comprehend God, our limited language cannot accurately illustrate the details of God.

The imagination of a child is limitless. Children describe God using language and images with which they are familiar. As adults, we know there is no true way to describe God to others. So, we rely on our faith and experience to talk about an indescribable Creator to those who question God's existence, character, and nature.

When you were a child, what did you imagine God looked like? What about now? Get creative by drawing what you think God looks like in the space.

Katie Shockley is a licensed local pastor in The United Methodist Church. Katie and her husband Steve are full-time RVers, traveling across the country with their two cats.

The Seventh Day

BY ABBY HAILEY

Keep the Sabbath day and treat it as holy, exactly as the LORD your God commanded: Six days you may work and do all your tasks, but the seventh day is a Sabbath to the LORD your God. Don't do any work on it—not you, your sons or daughters, your male or female servants, your oxen or donkeys or any of your animals, or the immigrant who is living among you—so that your male and female servants can rest just like you. Remember that you were a slave in Egypt, but the LORD your God brought you out of there with a strong hand and an outstretched arm. That's why the LORD your God commands you to keep the Sabbath day (Deuteronomy 5:12-15).

At a recent church council meeting, I posed a couple of questions: "What does Sabbath mean to you? What Sabbath practices are part of your life?" Awkward silence ensued. We had a hard time coming up with anything to say.

This seems a common response when it comes to the fourth commandment. It's the longest of the Ten Commandments, taking up four out of the twenty verses devoted to the commandments in Exodus 20, and four of the sixteen verses rehashing the commandments in Deuteronomy 5. The Sabbath commandment has been called by some the central hinge of the commandments, an indispensable bridge connecting the first three commandments that focus on relationship with God to the last six that center on relationship with neighbor.

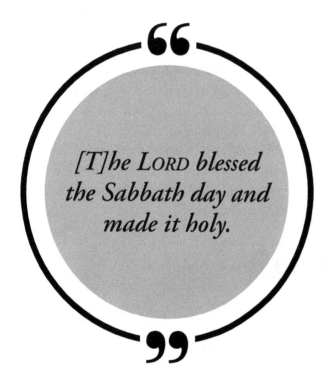

[T]he LORD blessed the Sabbath day and made it holy.

But as C. Christopher Smith and John Pattison point out in their book *Slow Church*, "The only one of the Ten Commandments we publicly brag about breaking is the one about remembering the sabbath and keeping it holy, [even though] we are never given any indication (in the Old Testament or New Testament) that forsaking the sabbath is any more or less justifiable than murder, theft and adultery."

Somehow, we have marked this commandment as less important or more dispensable than the rest. Perhaps God anticipated this, and this is the reason this is the only commandment God took time to explain.

In the Deuteronomy account, God tied the commandment to the story of the people's liberation, as they had been freed from relentless work in Egypt. For one day a week, all humans and animals alike would be set free from the tyranny of labor and given freedom to rest.

When the commandment was given in Exodus, however, it claimed even more ancient roots: "Because the LORD made the heavens and the earth, the sea, and everything that is in them in six days, but rested on the seventh day. That is why the LORD blessed the Sabbath day and made it holy" (Exodus 20:11).

Whichever explanation one turns to, the Sabbath is a way for God's people to remember who they are and where they've come from. By resting as God rests, by giving rest to our neighbors as God has given us rest, we are reminded each week of the character of the One who created us and called us into being as a people. By shaping our rhythm of life after God's own rhythm, we may be reshaped into the image of God in which we were created.

According to biblical scholar Walter Brueggeman in *Sabbath as Resistance* that the Creation account culminates not with the creation of humanity but with a day of rest tells us three things: that God is not a workaholic, that God is not anxious about creation, and that creation's continued existence and thriving does not depend on relentless work.

All three of these are things we need to be reminded today. American work culture could rarely be described as healthy. We are one of the few developed nations not to require paid annual leave. American workers log more hours annually

than counterparts in Great Britain, France, and Japan, among other developed nations. And the further down you are on the economic scale, the less likely you are to get any rest from work. Beyond this, in the age of constant accessibility to our phones and in-boxes, work is something we rarely set aside.

Anxiety is also a hallmark of our modern life. We hear Jesus' words, which carry echoes of God's rest: "Come to me, all you who are struggling hard and carrying heavy loads, and I will give you rest" (Matthew 11:28), but they sound to us like a pipe dream when we feel like we have to struggle so hard to provide for our families and our needs.

The idea of trusting God enough to rest? For most of us, that is much easier said than done. And many of us likely think the continued thriving of our world and those around us depends on our own relentless efforts. If we stop what we're doing for a minute, all those balls we've been juggling will fall to the ground and the whole world might crash to a halt!

But if God can rest, then surely we, created in God's image, are meant for rest.

It shows, as Brueggeman points out in *Genesis: Interpretation,* that God "is confident enough to rest. It was then and is now an assertion that life does not depend upon our feverish activity of self-securing, but that there can be a pause in which life is given to us simply as a gift."

If God is confident enough to rest, can't we demonstrate enough confidence in that God to rest from time to time too?

God, remind me that the world doesn't depend on me. It depends on you. Amen.

Abby Hailey is a native of Richmond, Virginia. She holds a master's of divinity from Duke Divinity School. Abby loves the ecumenical work of writing and editing curriculum for various publishers. Abby enjoys playing guitar, kayaking, and eagerly anticipating the start of a new Duke basketball season.

Dig into Gardening Trends:
Tips to Get Started

Just like fashion, trends in gardening come and go . . . and sometimes come back again. Some shifts in gardening were inspired by necessity, like the "victory gardens" of WWII for growing food during years of rationing. Others reflected societal changes, like the green lawns of the 1950s and 1960s, when families spent more time playing and entertaining in their yards than ever before. If you look further into the past, to the 1920s, you see a trend that's on the rise again—a yearning for going back to nature, celebrating a lush, green, and bird-friendly environment.

Those 1920s gardens overflowed with all sorts of greenery, fishponds, birdbaths, and bird feeders.

Today's interest in sustainable gardens offering a home for pollinators is not too different from the desire for bird-watching and natural gardening of one hundred years ago.

A new survey by the National Garden Bureau (NGB), which is celebrating its 100th anniversary, found fascinating trends among today's gardeners, both expert and novice, which may inspire ideas for your own gardens.

Grow to Eat

More than half (57%) of those age 35 and under said they're using their green space to grow their own food. That interest was echoed by respondents over 35, with 65% of them saying they planned to turn at least part of their future gardens into more of a food source. Many expressed interest in growing their own herbs in their kitchens, with many respondents sharing plans to grow herbs indoors in the future.

New to growing veggies, fruits, or herbs? Consider starting seeds in your kitchen or creating a small raised garden bed outdoors. Research what grows best in your region and the most ideal time for planting. Start small, with just one or two types of plants, so you don't feel overwhelmed. And grow something you know you'll love to eat!

Mixed-use Gardens

Gardens past and present have served multiple purposes, and gardening with a variety of plants allows you to enjoy your space and take in the outdoors to your liking. Many respondents shared that while they want some green lawn, they also want the rest of their yard to be planted with trees, shrubs, flowers, fruits, herbs, and vegetables.

What does that mean for gardens of the future? They'll likely offer more variety, from the ornamental to the edible.

Over 60% of gardeners of all ages want to grow pollinator-friendly plants and flowers.

Look at your own yard and decide how much of it you want to dedicate to your garden and containers, or perhaps what other types of plants you could grow instead. Consider consulting a professional in your area as a resource for advice on a strategy for your space.

Victory Garden 2.0

When the *Victory Garden Manual* was first written in 1943, reasons to grow your own vegetables were obvious: it was wartime and food was scarce. Statistics say that in 1943, nearly 40% of all fruits and vegetables grown in the US were grown in home and community victory gardens.

As NGB celebrates its 100th anniversary, it seems timely to reintroduce the concept of victory gardening with quick and easy steps to plan and grow your own vegetable garden. Before digging in, it may be helpful to create a list of vegetables that your family enjoys. From there, plan your garden space and determine if you'll be planting in the ground, raised beds, containers, or a combination. Don't forget to add pollinator-friendly flowers to ensure vegetables are properly pollinated, and you'll have a great start on the modern victory garden.

Growing Inspiration

The internet can be a great source of inspiration for future gardeners. While gardeners can look to magazines, books, and garden retailers for ideas, don't forget about browsing Pinterest, Instagram, and YouTube for information and tips about developing your green thumb. Talk to friends and family for ideas and inspiration about what, and how, to grow.

For more information, tips, blogs, and lots of inspiring gardening ideas, visit *ngb.org*.

Source: Brandpoint

How You Walk Through the World:

Tips for Staying Safe While Traveling

BY SUSAN SALLEY

You're walking down a street in Barcelona—in the dream, you blend in, you're part of the parade, you're at ease. But how do you join the scenery and not look like what you most likely are: a tourist or at least a visitor?

Security boosts your confidence and helps you do all that you hope to do in a strange city. There are also practical tips that fellow travelers can offer that do boost your safety. Part of being and feeling safe is not sending out the signals that you are out of place, unsure of yourself, distracted, or inattentive.

Barcelona comes to mind because Las Ramblas is the most recent place where I didn't feel safe, and I wanted to go back to the hotel. I knew the area was prone to pickpockets, and I felt like a target. Luckily, I had been warned (and by savvy travelers who never overreact!). I had taken precautions, and I was fine, but I didn't like the feeling! You can do simple things to take care. I asked some friends who travel often to share their best ideas.

How You Look

Posture. How *do* you walk through the world? Looking both in control and aware makes you a less obvious target. My good friend, Beth, has terrific posture. She says, "Whenever I am in a situation where I feel vulnerable, I straighten my spine, throw back my shoulders, and channel my inner force field." Confidence, strength, and focus make a difference.

Blending in. Look around when you arrive in a city. How do people dress? How do they carry their belongings? Are there ways you can easily change your appearance to blend in?

What you carry. If you can, no maps, no backpacks. You might stop for coffee and get your bearings with your map at a table, but not in front of your face on the street. I have come to love using the map app on my phone, but I don't walk along staring at my phone. Look up and around you. Get the route and put the phone away.

Attentiveness. Don't stroll the streets staring at your phone, and don't you dare wear earbuds.

What You Do

Ask for help smartly. Lisa Ball of Lisa Ball Travel Design in Kansas City is beyond savvy. She says, "Know who to ask for help. If you're lost in a city, go inside a reputable hotel. Hotels always have maps and usually a nice person who will give directions."

Remember the little things. Look for small things you can do. In Paris, so many residents use metro passes, and I find the smaller station's ticket machines sometimes out of order. I buy more than a single ticket and keep an extra or two. Keep a little easily-accessible cash in your pocket for the small things. Carry a card or brochure from your hotel to show taxi drivers in case your pronunciation is as bad as mine.

Care for your financial security. Another friend, Cliff, once asked why I was stressed about packing. "All you need, really," he said, "is your passport and credit card." To some degree, he's right. Here are things I do to secure those:

- Take your debit card and at least two credit cards. Check them for damage. Really. You may forget that your debit card has a little crack until it gets remarkably worse . . . in Istanbul. Call your card companies and make sure they know your travel dates and destinations so you won't be surprised by fraud alerts and freezes.
- Don't carry all your cards and cash with you. I leave a card and cash locked in my suitcase or in the room safe when I am out and about.

- Copy or photograph the front and back of your cards and stash them somewhere separate just in case you need to cancel a card.
- Recently, I signed up for Venmo, a mobile app that allows people to send you money using your phone number or email address. If something goes wrong, a quick way for friends or family to send you cash is good.
- Also, scan and email a copy of your passport to yourself, as well as tucking a print copy in your luggage.

Have quick and easy access to your travel information. I still go old school and print out my spreadsheet (yes, it is true) with my confirmation numbers, prepayments, train and plane information. I also email this to myself so I can retrieve it digitally.

Travel light. A woman in heels with too many bags doesn't just look like a target, she is. If you are traveling alone, travel light and smart. Once settled in, I never carry a normal purse when I'm alone. Use a small bag under your jacket or good cross-body bag that you can slide to the front.

My friend, Susan, travels solo in a different way for her work. She does a lot of driving between small towns in the US, often leaving her hotel before dawn. Her advice is wise whether you are in the next state or across the globe:

1. I wear my work uniform—a white lab coat—when I walk around. I know most people don't have this prop, but it gives me an air of someone of importance.
2. I ALWAYS have my keys in hand (hotel room, car) when I exit the hotel or vehicle.
3. I keep a large tote in my car so that I can consolidate the items I am carrying in and out of hotels (my purse, food, drink, etc.), so I'm not fumbling with a lot of separate bags.
4. I park as close to the entrance as I can. I often am working at 4:00 a.m., and I'm supposed to park in the outer parking areas, but I don't. I always park very close and then move my car after daylight.

There is great advice online from people who travel, including choosing your room, safety inside hotels, and taking transportation. Being aware and doing some reading can give you both greater safety and greater confidence.

Tips to Feel Safe

- Make it **personal**. We are all different, so what causes you stress? Make a list of your top three stressors, and then construct clear plans to address *your* list.
- If you feel insecure and are flustered, **stop**. Find a restaurant, hotel, or good shop. Stop and compose yourself. You are more vulnerable when you are off-balance.
- Pick your **home base** with care. I know that on my list is having a zone of space in a city where I feel at ease, can take a late walk, and feel like I can travel without armor. I will pay more for a small single in a hotel or inn with good staff in a great neighborhood for this—and make up the cost in some picnic dinners and less shopping.

Susan Salley is an associate publisher at Abingdon Press. A former tour agent and avid traveler, she blogs at www.solo-travel.com.

The Voice of the Author

BY SCOTT SPRADLEY

I'm a big fan of audiobooks. I listen to a little bit of everything: classic and popular fiction, thrillers, business, health, personal development, biographies, and of course, spiritual books. I confess that in the popular fiction and thriller categories, I have my favorite voice actors. But in the nonfiction categories, I always prefer the voice of the author. In my mind, hearing the author read their own book gives me a much better picture of what they meant and how they felt when they said something, and if they are writing what they truly believe.

During the quarantine of 2020, I listened to the late Maya Angelou reading, *I Know Why the Caged Bird Sings.* Listening to Dr. Angelou tell this story of her life in her own voice is an experience beyond description, and I savored every moment of it.

One of the reasons I answered the call into Spiritual Direction is because I know God is still speaking to us, and I believe that no one is excluded from hearing the loving voice of the Author of our lives, no one. A favorite story of mine is found in the first three Gospels: the baptism of Jesus. The part that really touches me is when God's voice is heard claiming Jesus as beloved Son, with whom God is well pleased or in whom God finds happiness. To me, it is remarkable that three different accounts of this story report God's voice being heard. And I love the message.

I'm sure biblical scholars hold differing opinions on why and how this happened and how it ended up in three of four canonical Gospels. But in my opinion, it is in these books of the Bible because it gives one of the truest pictures of how God feels about us as God's children, Jesus, and the entire human race. I think the Author of our lives wants us all to know that we belong as God's children and that God is pleased with us, or finds happiness in us, just because we were created and we exist. If you take the time to re-read these accounts of this story and note what comes before and after, you'll see that God said these loving words before Jesus began what we know of as his earthly mission. So, before Jesus did anything notable in the Bible, God was pleased with him and claimed him as God's own.

There are a lot of voices out there speaking on behalf of the Author of our lives. It is tempting to listen to what "experts" or "authorities" have to say on God's behalf and just go with those ideas and opinions. But I truly believe that each one of us is capable of hearing the Author's voice. I believe that God, the Author, is already speaking to us in ways we may or may not have learned to hear. So, if you are like so many of us, and you find yourself seeking and longing to know God's will for your life and for the power to carry it out, why not put some effort into listening for and learning to hear God's voice for yourself?

I expect there are as many ways of hearing God's voice as there are people trying to listen. But here are a few ways that have been helpful to me.

In Scripture, Poetry, Music, or Other Forms of the Written Word—The go-to move for many of us with Scripture is to try and interpret what is written or said. Though there's nothing wrong with that approach, why not let Scripture, poetry, and music read us? This can be done with multiple slow readings and standard Lectio Divina questions like, "What word or phrase stands out to me? Where does what I am hearing intersect with or connect to what's happening in my life right now? What might God be inviting me to as I experience these words?"

We can also engage our five senses as we encounter the written, spoken, or sung word. Trusting the gift of imagination God has given you, take notice of sights, sounds, smells, tastes, and bodily sensations you experience as you engage the material.

In the Details of Our Daily Lives—Often, God shows up in our everyday lives in ways we may not consider to be divine communication. In Spiritual Direction sessions, directees and directors often look through the details of the past week or month, noting the highs, lows, and even the mundane. Taking the time to recount these events to another person or even in a journal often reveals words God wants to say to us or things God wants us to pay attention to. Words or things that, in the moment, we may have missed. Ask helpful questions like, "Where do I notice God's grace in this? What do I need to learn from this? How does this make me feel about God? What does this say about how God is present to me?"

In Dreams—Though that pizza I had an hour before bedtime and the movie I was watching may have provided some raw materials for my imagination to work with, dreams are much more than the byproduct of poor decisions before bedtime. Throughout the Bible, we find examples of God speaking to God's children through dreams and visions (often called "waking dreams"). It has been my experience that God is still speaking to us through dreams and visions. A number of great books on dreamwork (and even some good courses and retreats) can help you learn to understand the ways God might be speaking to you through the gifts of nighttime dreams.

Though hearing God speak to us may take effort, the assurance it can give is priceless. Hearing the Author's voice, knowing God is speaking to you, and discerning what God is inviting you to do might be something you long for. It may seem way beyond what you believe you can experience alone with God. This is not a journey to be taken alone. Though reliance on experts may get in the way of our hearing God's voice, inviting a guide, friend, or spiritual director on the journey with us can be eye-opening (or in this case, ear-opening) and fulfilling. As Matthew 18:20 tells us, "For where two or three are gathered in my name, I'm there with them."

If you don't believe you've heard the Author's voice and you wonder what God might be saying to you, I hope and pray you will take the time and effort to listen, and I hope you'll take a chance on believing that God loves you enough to speak straight to your soul.

May you know God's nearness and hear God's loving voice speak to you as you are on this journey, and may you journey in good company.

_____

A practicing Spiritual Director since 2013, Scott Spradley received his certification in Spiritual Direction from Perkins School of Theology. Scott also serves as Director for the VBS team at The United Methodist Publishing House. Scott, his wife, and his son attend Providence United Methodist Church in Mt. Juliet, Tennessee, and live in Smyrna, Tennessee. For more info: www.spradleyspiritualdirection.com.

Tips to Recognize Ripe Fruits

Keeping fresh fruit around the house provides a healthier alternative when your sweet tooth comes calling. Understanding how and when to buy at the peak of ripeness (or just before, in some cases) can help you avoid food waste while keeping your doctor happy.

Consider these simple tips for recognizing ripe fruits:

- **Strawberries:** Check the area at the top of the berry near the stem and leaves. A ripe strawberry is fully red; green or white near the top means the fruit is underripe.
- **Watermelon:** The "field spot," or the area where the melon sat on the ground, should be yellow, and a tap on the rind should produce a hollow sound.
- **Cherries:** Flesh should appear dark with a crimson color and feel firm.
- **Blueberries:** Similar to cherries, color should deepen to dark blue. A reddish or pink color may be visible in unripe berries.
- **Blackberries:** Look for a smooth texture without any red appearance. Because blackberries don't ripen after being picked, they tend to spoil quickly.
- **Cantaloupe:** You should detect a sweet smell, and the melon should feel heavy upon lifting.

- **Peaches:** A sweet, fragrant odor should be apparent. Skin should feel tender but not soft.
- **Pineapple:** Smell is again an important factor for pineapple   a sweet scent shows it's ready, but a vinegary one likely means it's overripe.
- **Raspberries:** Generally follow the same rules as blackberries. Best eaten within a couple days of purchase; a bright red color represents ripe berries.
- **Bananas:** A ripe banana features a peel lightly spotted without significant bruising. Your best bet may be to purchase bananas still slightly green and allow them to ripen at home.

Find more food tips, tricks, recipes, and videos at *www.Culinary.net.*

Source: Family Features

Super Snacking

Snacks are a way of life for people of all ages according to research published in the *Journal of Nutrition Education and Behavior*. Having nutritionally-balanced snacks on hand at home can make for a happy and healthy day.

Planning snacks that are as delicious as they are healthy is a winning solution, and snacks are a simple way to add more nutrition to your diet.

For example, low-fat and fat-free dairy foods are essential to growth and overall wellness. They provide calcium and vitamin D, two nutrients most people don't get enough of, according to the 2015 Dietary Guidelines for Americans. The guidelines recommend two to three servings of low-fat and fat-free dairy foods every day.

These recipes are all easy enough that adults or even kids can make them on their own (or with minimal assistance). Giving your grandkids the ability to play a role in the kitchen is a gift that can last a lifetime. The culinary skills they develop early in life can give them the confidence and know-how to cook nutritious meals for themselves as teens and adults.

Get more ideas to get you and your grandkids cooking and snacking smart at *milkmeansmore.org*.

Red, White, and Blue Greek Yogurt Bark

Prep time: 5 minutes
Servings: 12

- 3 cups plain non-fat Greek yogurt
- 1/3 cup honey, plus additional for drizzling (optional)
- 1 teaspoon vanilla
- 1/2 cup strawberries, sliced into rounds
- 1/2 cup blueberries
- 1/2 cup raspberries, halved

In medium mixing bowl, combine Greek yogurt, 1/3 cup honey, and vanilla.

On parchment paper-lined baking sheet, spread Greek yogurt mixture to quarter-inch thickness. Press strawberries, blueberries, and raspberries into yogurt. Freeze at least three hours. Break into pieces upon removing from freezer.

Frozen Banana Pops
Servings: 8

4 large bananas, peeled
8 wooden ice pop sticks
2 cups vanilla non-fat Greek yogurt
1/2 cup creamy natural peanut butter

Cut each banana in half and carefully insert wooden ice pop stick in bottom of each, about one-third into banana. Place bananas on large baking sheet lined with parchment paper. Freeze bananas until partially frozen, about 30 minutes.

Carefully dip each banana in tall pint glass of vanilla yogurt to coat, leaving a half inch at bottom of banana uncoated. Return yogurt-coated bananas to parchment paper-lined baking sheet and freeze until completely firm, about one hour.

Microwave peanut butter until smooth and creamy, about 30–45 seconds. Drizzle peanut butter evenly over bananas, then place on baking sheet to freeze until peanut butter is firm, about 30 minutes.

Serve immediately or wrap each banana in plastic wrap and store in freezer up to three months.

Peanut Butter Yogurt Dip
Prep time: 5 minutes
Servings: 4

3/4 cup vanilla Greek yogurt
1/4 cup peanut butter
1 dash cinnamon
apples, graham crackers, or other dipper of
    choice

In bowl, mix Greek yogurt, peanut butter, and cinnamon until smooth.

Serve with apples, graham crackers, or another dipper of choice.

Good Morning Yogurt Parfait
Prep time: 5 minutes
Servings: 1

1/2 cup sliced or diced fruit, any variety
6 ounces low-fat or fat-free vanilla yogurt
1/4 cup granola or other cereal (optional)

In small bowl or cup, layer fruit and yogurt, starting with fruit on bottom. Top with cereal or granola, if desired.

Note: This recipe can be made using low-fat or non-fat cottage cheese sweetened with honey and cinnamon.

Source: Family Features

Cook Comfort Food *Once,* Enjoy It *Twice*

Cook once, eat twice. It's a kitchen practice as simple as it sounds. Cook a base dish that can be enjoyed today and used for an entirely different meal tomorrow. For example, bake some fish for tonight's dinner, and enjoy fish tacos for tomorrow's lunch.

Whether your love for cooking runs deep or is being newly discovered, keep the following in mind when planning to cook once and eat twice.

Stock up on staples. Before heading out to the store, develop a list of ingredients that can be used for multiple dishes. Canned goods, such as black beans and corn, are great items to store in the pantry and have on hand for a variety of favorite family recipes. Other basics like corn tortillas can be used in multiple ways, such as tacos, casseroles, and even salads.

Don't forget produce. To increase flavor and nutrition, adding produce is key in your planning. Mushrooms are a favorite among chefs and home cooks alike for many reasons. Traditionally known for their inherent umami flavor, mushrooms are filling, healthy, and versatile.

Make meat go further. A three-step cooking technique called "The Blend" combines finely chopped mushrooms with ground meat to create dishes that are more nutritious while still tasting delicious. You can use the process to create multiple dishes, such as tacos, pasta sauce, and burgers. Mushrooms' ability to mimic the texture of meat makes them easy to incorporate, and the addition of finely chopped mushrooms to meat dishes stretches portions, allowing the family to enjoy a meat-mushroom base two days in a row in two different ways in dishes like Mexican Lasagna and Blended Tacos, both of which include a Mexican Mushroom-Beef Blend.

For more simple and delicious recipes, visit *MushroomCouncil.com.*

Blended Tacos
Makes: 8 tacos

1 cup sour cream
6 tablespoons cilantro, chopped
2 tablespoons lime juice
8 yellow corn tortillas
2 cups Mexican Mushroom-Beef Blend
diced avocado (optional)
shredded lettuce (optional)
shredded cheese (optional)
salsa (optional)

In small bowl, mix sour cream, cilantro, and lime juice. Cover and refrigerate.

Warm tortillas in microwave or on stove top according to package directions. Spoon 1/4 cup Mexican Mushroom-Beef Blend into each tortilla. Top with sour cream mixture and avocado, lettuce, and cheese as desired.

Mexican Mushroom-Beef Blend
Makes: 8 cups

1 medium yellow onion
8 ounces fresh button or cremini mushrooms
1 pound lean ground beef
1 tablespoon olive oil
2 cans (15 ounces each) black beans, drained
1 package (1 ounce) reduced-sodium taco seasoning mix
1 can (15 ounces) crushed tomatoes
1 can (11 ounces) yellow kernel corn, drained

In food processor, pulse onion and mushrooms to coarse texture. Set aside.

In large frying pan, brown ground beef. Drain fat. Set aside.

In same frying pan, heat oil. Add mushroom mixture and sauté 3–4 minutes or until most moisture has been released. Add black beans and mix.

Add beef, taco seasoning, tomatoes, and corn to black bean and mushroom blend. Mix and cook until heated through.

Mexican Lasagna
Servings: 6–8

nonstick cooking spray
16 yellow corn tortillas
6 cups Mexican Mushroom-Beef Blend
1 cup shredded, low-fat Mexican cheese blend
sour cream (optional)
chopped cilantro (optional)
salsa (optional)

Heat oven to 350 F. Spray bottom of 9-by-13 baking dish with nonstick cooking spray. Place four corn tortillas on bottom of dish and layer 2 cups Mexican Mushroom-Beef Blend on top. Repeat layers, ending with tortillas as top layer. Top with cheese.

Bake uncovered 25 minutes or until cheese melts and lasagna is heated through. Top with dollops of sour cream, cilantro, and salsa as desired.

Source: Family Features

Live from Louisville

BY RACHEL MULLEN

It's a humid summer day. I hear the crack of the bat, oohs and aahs from the crowd. I'm not at the ballpark, though. I'm at the Louisville Slugger Museum & Factory in downtown Louisville, Kentucky. The museum and factory tour is a must-do for any fan of America's Favorite Pastime. Visitors can view bats custom-made for their favorite players, get a behind-the-scenes look at how the bats are made, and even swing an authentic Louisville Slugger for a stadium selfie.

Louisville has a lot to offer sports fans, whether they watch baseball, enjoy boxing, or like rooting on their favorite steed in the Kentucky Derby. In addition to the Louisville Slugger Museum & Factory, Louisville is home to the Minor League Baseball team, the Louisville Bats. The Bats play all summer, and tickets are quite affordable. Visit *www.milb.com/louisville* to see the schedule and find more information.

Fans of the sport of boxing don't want to miss the Muhammad Ali Center (walking distance from the Louisville Slugger Museum). A native son of Louisville, Ali was not only the boxing heavyweight champion of the world, but a successful musician, activist, and philanthropist. The Muhammad Ali Center highlights his many achievements through a variety of multimedia exhibits. There are six pavilions inside the museum, each highlighting a core principle of Ali's life: confidence, conviction, dedication, giving, respect, and spirituality.

If you know about one sporting event in Louisville, it's probably the Kentucky Derby. This annual event has been running in Louisville since 1875 on the first Saturday in May. The day before the Derby is the second-largest racing event in the city: the Kentucky Oaks (a race exclusively for fillies). Churchill

Photo: Thomas Kelley/Shutterstock.com

Downs, home to both the Derby and the Oaks, is arguably the most famous horse-racing track in the world. While the Derby is in May, the Kentucky Derby Museum is open year-round. Visitors can tour two floors of exhibits about the famous race and take a guided tour of Churchill Downs Racetrack. A recent addition to the museum is the resident thoroughbred and pony that you can see in a new stable area.

The Brown Hotel is the crown jewel of lodging in Louisville. The Brown opened its doors in 1923, a lavish testament to Georgian-Revival elegance popular at the time. This stately property is listed on the National Registry of Historic Places, so even if you don't stay overnight, be sure to check out the ornate common areas. There is often live music in the lobby, and you can't go wrong dining at any of the restaurants on-site.

It was at The Brown Hotel that one of Kentucky's most famous dishes was created: the Hot Brown. Fortunately, it's much more delicious than it sounds. Originally created as a late-night snack for dance patrons, the Hot Brown is an open-faced turkey sandwich with bacon, cheese, and Mornay sauce served piping hot. Every restaurant in the hotel serves the sandwich, as do countless restaurants across Louisville.

To understand what makes Louisville's park system so impressive, it helps to take a look at the man who designed it: Frederick Law Olmsted. Olmsted (1822–1903) was the landscape architect behind some of our nation's most famous public spaces and is considered to be the father of American landscape architecture. He co-designed Central Park in New York City; was involved in creating the country's oldest state park, The Niagara Reservation at Niagara Falls; worked on the US Capitol and Biltmore Estate grounds; and designed the entire parks and parkway system in Louisville, Kentucky. The Louisville park system was the last he created, and according to locals, the crown jewel of his long, illustrious career. Olmsted was invited to Louisville in 1891 and tasked with creating three parks in different parts of the city and a system of parkways to connect them. In addition to the large parks (Cherokee, Iroquois, and Shawnee), Olmsted's firm created smaller parks and playgrounds throughout the city (eighteen in total), which are still open today.

The day I chose to visit Cherokee Park was a drizzly one. The rain added to the humidity to make for a very unpleasant hiking experience. Fortunately, the park can be easily enjoyed from the comfort of a car. There is a 2.5-mile scenic loop through the park that showcases its many beautiful natural features. Bubbling streams, rolling hills, and wide-open meadows surrounded me. Even the neighborhoods just outside the park were worth driving through. Historic homes and churches made for the perfect conclusion to my driving tour.

One specific historic home I had to see while in Louisville was the Conrad-Caldwell House Museum. Constructed in 1895 by Louisville architect Arthur Loomis, this Richardsonian Romanesque castle shines bright in the city that claims to have the largest concentration of Victorian homes in the country. Guided tours take place throughout the day and offer behind-the-scenes insight into this magnificent home.

I checked out of my room at The Brown Hotel, stopping in the gift shop to gawk at over-the-top Derby hats one last time. My visit to Louisville was full of sport, history, and nature. I considered it to be a real home run!

Rachel Mullen is the Features and Acquisitions Editor for Christian Living in the Mature Years.

Photo: Joe Hendrickson/Shutterstock.com

BY ANGELA REISS

The Impulse to Share

I enjoy re-creating and re-purposing things, creating something new from something old. Several years ago, I decided to try something crazy and join about 150 million other people in the blogging world. I shared pictures and details about all the items I found at yard sales and thrift stores and had transformed. At first, it was really exciting. I was creating and writing. I learned a little bit about coding and reintroduced myself to graphic design. I don't know that I was ever really good at any of it, but I enjoyed how all of those things met together at this one place that was a creative representation of me.

The blogging world is filled with appreciators and collectors of cleverness and creative thought. I thought about that as I read Acts 17. I imagined Paul walking through the city of Athens, looking at all of the idols and the altars for every god and goddess people thought might possibly exist, even one someone had constructed for an unknown god. I could see him becoming visibly shocked by what he saw, so much that it stirred him to action. I remember how I felt when I sat at my desk poring over the blogs of other women. It stirred me to action, but of a different kind than Paul. I got caught up in the frenzy of comparison and wanting to impress people. I wanted to be the one who had the cleverest thoughts and the most creative transformations. I wasn't that person, but I wanted to be.

Over the course of the next year, I began to feel a heaviness in my heart. And it got heavier each time I published a blog post. I began to feel like the gifts that God had given me to create beauty were contributing to peoples' desires to possess more material things. I was advocating for something that I didn't believe in, and it made me feel empty.

And that was my fault. I shared the details of what I was doing, of the item's restoration and beauty. But I didn't share or invite people into how God used that item to continue to bring restorative healing to my life. It always felt more intimate than I was comfortable sharing with the world.

In Acts 17, we read about Paul's insistence that idolatry is rooted in ignorance and how now that God has revealed God's self, God would no longer be okay with people claiming ignorance. And I think that's where the heaviness in my heart was coming from. I knew that each blog post contributed to comparison and materialism and not to furthering the kingdom of heaven. So, I really had to ask myself why I was still willing to click that publish button. It was a question that caused me to repent and shut it all down and walk away from the blogging world.

It still kind of takes my breath away that not much time passed before God held a door wide open for me to walk through. I began working at a church in children's ministry, where I get to create and write. I get to do graphic design and use every single one of the gifts God has given me. And I can't express to you how full I feel and how much joy it brings to my heart to see how all those things come together at this one place that is a creative representation of God.

"God, who made the world and everything in it, is Lord of heaven and earth. He doesn't live in temples made with human hands," Paul told the people of Athens. "Nor is God served by human hands, as though he needed something, since he is the one who gives life, breath, and everything else. . . . In God we live, move, and exist" (Acts 17:24-25, 28).

Angela Reiss is a pastor on staff at Providence United Methodist Church in Mount Juliet, Tennessee. Angela is passionate about walking with Jesus and living out the life God has called her to: helping people disconnected from God and the church find hope, healing, and wholeness in Jesus Christ. Angela is smitten with her husband, Damon, and together they cheer on their three full-of-life children.

The Long Road

BY BEN HOWARD

There are a lot of stories in the Christian tradition about what happened to the apostles after Jesus' ascension. The most colorful is probably the one about Peter being crucified upside down by the Roman Emperor Nero because he felt he was unworthy to die in the same way as Christ. It's certainly a powerful story, but it's not the one that most captures my imagination. I'm most fascinated by the stories about the apostles' travels after Jesus' ministry and the spread of the gospel.

According to Christian tradition, Andrew traveled all the way to modern-day Russia carrying the gospel to the people who lived there. He's often recognized as the most important saint in the Russian Orthodox Church. There's also the story of Thomas, who was said to travel to India. Even today, two thousand years later, there is a strain of Indian Christianity called the Mar Thoma Church, that traces its lineage to Thomas's missionary journey.

Today we travel all over the world and do so at speeds that would boggle the minds of everyone in recorded history. That was not the case for disciples in the first century. In first-century Judea, it was probably a rare journey that took them farther than

Jerusalem. For reference, the distance from Nazareth to Jerusalem was about ninety miles. When your world has been that small for your entire life, how much of a risk is it to travel to Greece or Rome or Russia or India? When you've never been more than one hundred miles from home, what does it mean to set out on a journey of two or three or four thousand miles?

The best comparison we have today for this kind of commitment would be if someone asked you to go to Mars. Would you be willing to give up two years, three years, the rest of your life to do the work God had called you to do?

Jesus' call to the apostles was not a simple one. It was deeply disruptive, and it forced them to abandon the lives they grew up expecting to live. It's the same call we receive today. I pray that we embrace the challenge and let God lead us to do incredible things.

Benjamin Howard is an editor for Teaching and Learning Resources at The United Methodist Publishing House. He received his master's in Theological Studies from Lipscomb University and currently resides in Nashville, Tennessee.

Why Intergenerational Friendships Are Important

BY SELENA CUNNINGHAM

When I was just out of college, I asked my grandmother, "Do people ever feel the age they are on the inside?" "No," she replied. "You're always the same on the inside."

This was both a relief, as I had begun to worry about the fact that I was getting older but I still did not yet feel like a "grownup," and terrifying because I realized I would always feel on the inside like someone my outer appearance does not reflect. What would this mean in terms of how others perceived me?

Most of us, consciously or not, use outside appearance to decide who we will spend our time with. We tend to gravitate toward people our own age because they look like us. But the older I get, the more I realize we are all the same on the inside; some of us just have a little more life experience. We also need friendships with people of different ages. I'll tell you a couple of stories about how I came to realize this.

When I was in my twenties, I went through a phase where I was very into community-education writing classes. One summer, I attended a writers workshop at my local library. Early into this workshop, the facilitator asked us to pair up with another person and discuss types of books we liked to read (a book lover's icebreaker).

Most people there were older than me. There was only one person sort of close to my age, but obviously younger. The girl I paired with, Jill, was the angsty sort of teenager I had always been on the inside but never had the courage to be on the

outside when I was her age. Her short, boy-cut dark hair fell over one eye in such a way that she was able to give the perfect "Are you kidding me?" look without effort. She wore a great deal of black, various bracelets made out of leather and string on both arms, and heavy boots even in the heat of a Tennessee summer. From the start, I could tell that she was very uncomfortable with being in the room full of "old folks" (i.e. youngish-adult dreamers and late-life final-chance writers).

As we sat facing each other, cross-legged on the floor in a corner of the room, I wasn't sure Jill was going to actually talk to me. When she finally did, I learned that she was sent to the conference because her mom thought it would be good for her, but she wasn't all that into it. Surprising both of us, we learned that we had many common books in our reading histories. She was a fan of horror novels as I had been when I was younger. I had outgrown these favorite high school reads, but revisiting the stories from the perspective of a person who was just discovering them was nostalgic and fun!

Over the course of the conference, Jill and I became conference buddies. We participated in the same breakout groups and had lunch together. She became more open in conversations and actually smiled a couple of times. After the conference, Jill asked if we could exchange email addresses. We did, but honestly, I doubted I would ever hear from her again. After all, I was "old."

A few days later, I received a "What's up?" email from Jill. We wrote back and forth a few times, but to my own surprise, it was not Jill who fell down on the friendship job; it was me. I began to think, *I'm too old to be friends with someone her age,* and I let myself drift away.

Many years later, I realize that I missed an opportunity by dropping the ball on that friendship. It was true that I didn't need a friend so much younger than me, but obviously, Jill needed an older friend like me. Had I not let my discomfort with our age difference bother me, I could have served in a mentor or big sister role to her, but I couldn't see that then. And whether I knew it or not, the friendship could have benefited me too. It would have forced me to look at a reflection of my younger inner self on a regular basis. That self dreamed of writing great things, but in truth, got lost along the way as life's responsibilities replaced dreams. I sometimes wonder what happened to Jill. I pray that she turned out okay and found good friends along the way, and that my friendship letdown did not affect her too much.

Fast-forward a few years, and I was ready to shake up my whole life by quitting my office job and going back to school. I decided to pursue a master's degree in English. To do so, I needed a more flexible schedule. So, I traded in my comfy cubicle chair for standing all day in an upscale home furnishings showroom (crazy, I know).

On my first day, I showed up to work in a pink blouse, tan A-line skirt, and heels. The manager introduced me to my fellow salespeople:

a wiry-looking, middle-aged man named Alvin; and a tall, gray-haired woman named Martha who proudly told me she was retired but worked there to stay busy. Shamefully, I admit that I made some assumptions about my coworkers' ages. My first thought was, *Well, it looks like I'm going to be carrying a lot of stuff to cars for people.* Boy, was I wrong! Those two were in better shape than many people half their age. However, I wasn't the only one drawing wrong conclusions based on appearance.

On that first day, as we all stood at the counter watching customers mill about, pondering the right moment to swoop in for the sale, Martha turned to me, looked me up and down, and said, "Those shoes aren't going to work here."

At this point, I decided that Martha was going to be my enemy.

I straightened my back, stood firmly on those heels, and said to her, "This is what I have right now, so they'll have to do."

Of course, Martha was right (though I'd never admit it), but what she didn't know was that I was still working at my office job and had come straight from one job to the other. At the same time, school was already starting, and the furthest thing from my mind was shopping for shoes, sensible or otherwise. Just as I had stereotyped her, she had stereotyped me.

I would quickly learn that by my clothing, she assumed I had never done a day of hard work in my life and would not last long. And she soon told me, "You will never find a husband if you take an advanced degree." Well, I was no stranger to retail or hard work, and I had a serious boyfriend I wasn't inclined to tell Martha about just yet.

Yes, I thought, *this woman will be my enemy.*

After a few months, I learned that Martha lived in a nearby suburb, and she learned that it was my hometown. Her grandchildren were the same ages as my niece and nephew. We also realized that we enjoyed some of the same television shows, and introduced each other to a few as well. And most

importantly, we both had excellent taste in home furnishings!

Not a year later, it would be Martha who would stand up for me when snooty customers would snub me because I was the youngest on staff.

My enemy was now Martha's enemy.

Who would have thought three years later, when I graduated with that husband-deterring degree, Martha would be the one to orchestrate the only break-room celebration I have ever seen with fine linens and china? And when I got engaged, it was Martha with whom I'd spend the day talking over wedding ideas. Yet, when that relationship failed and the engagement was called off, without a question, Martha's response was, "Well, good." This, to me, represented the mark of a true friend, a person who supports you no matter what.

Over the years, we'd vented about work, talked over world events, and worried and rejoiced together over family and personal matters. Who would have thought two women nearly forty years apart in age would have found such common ground?

Though the business we worked for closed, and Martha and I moved on and drifted apart over time, we still remained friends. If you asked me on that first day of working together if Martha and I would be exchanging Christmas cards so many years later, I would have said, "No way." I am so glad I was wrong!

Through these relationships, I learned that intergenerational friendships have many benefits both for younger and older people.

Knowledge

- For younger people, such relationships are the source of invaluable wisdom and advice.
- For older people, intergenerational friendships can offer introductions to new and unexpected interests, and a connection to current events and technologies that might otherwise be left unexplored.
- These relationships present opportunities for learning for both parties.

Community

- Intergenerational relationships help build stronger communities by promoting mutual respect and understanding between people in different age groups who interact through working, serving, and worshipping.
- They also help ensure that history, experiences, and wisdom are passed down to future generations.
- Intergenerational relationships also help build stronger family relationships. By getting to know people outside of our families who are older or younger than us, we build a sense of understanding that can help us see our family members of different ages in a different light and relate to them better as individuals, rather than just as the role they play in the family (i.e., parent, grandparent, aunt, or uncle).

Quality of Life

- It is often said that younger people keep older people young.
- Older people also enrich the lives of younger people by sharing stories and experiences that would be missing from their lives if they only associated with their peers.
- Both parties experience an overall richer life experience from interacting with each other.

Selena Cunningham is an editor, writer, and educator who lives in Franklin, Tennessee. She enjoys learning new things, spending time with family and friends, and experiencing good stories.

The Undiscussed Medical Error

While you may routinely hear about medical errors, it's less common to hear about a misdiagnosis. Inaccurate or delayed medical diagnosis is a medical error many people rarely talk about. Yet, research released by the Society to Improve Diagnosis in Medicine (SIDM) shows it remains the most common, costly, and catastrophic of all medical errors.

Researchers at Johns Hopkins Medicine and CRICO Strategies found that 34% of malpractice cases resulting in death or permanent disability stem from an inaccurate or delayed diagnosis, making it the number-one cause of serious harm among medical errors.

This happens, in large part, because making and communicating a medical diagnosis is a complex and imperfect science. There are more than 10,000 known diseases and more than 5,000 laboratory tests, but only a limited number of symptoms to provide the clues necessary to make an accurate diagnosis.

However, there is a new sense of momentum in the healthcare community to raise awareness and reduce inaccurate and delayed diagnoses, including more funding from the federal government.

Even as researchers and experts continue to explore how best to address this costly, dangerous, and sometimes deadly issue, it is important for patients to be aware of it. Everyone has a role to play in improving the diagnostic process, including physicians, nurses, radiologists, laboratory scientists, health system leaders, and, perhaps most especially, patients.

It's critically important that patients share information with their medical providers and know the right questions to ask in order to decrease the likelihood of misdiagnosis.

To help patients have conversations with their physicians about their diagnoses, SIDM's patient toolkit offers a questions checklist, including these seven questions to ask:

1. **What is my diagnosis? What else could it be?**
2. **Why do you think this is my diagnosis? From test results? From my physical exam?**
3. **Can you give me written information about my diagnosis? A pamphlet? A website?**
4. **Can you explain the test or treatment you want me to have?**
5. **What are the risks to the test or treatment you want me to have? What happens if I do nothing?**
6. **When do I need to follow up with you?**
7. **What should I do if my symptoms worsen or change, or if I don't respond to treatment?**

In addition to these questions, always ask when test results will be ready. Get a copy for your records, and call your doctor's office if you do not receive your test results.

For more information and steps you can take to avoid misdiagnosis, download the Patient's Toolkit for Diagnosis and share your personal story of inaccurate or delayed diagnosis at *ImproveDiagnosis.org.*

Source: Family Features

Find the Differences

Look at the two illustrations below. Find and circle the 11 differences between the two.

Answer key is on page 50.

Answers to the puzzle on page 49.

The story of the tower of Babel appears in the first book of the Bible, Genesis. Dive deep into this all-important book with the *Genesis to Revelation* Bible study. This study of the entire Book of Genesis begins with the Creation story and ends with Jacob and his family reuniting. *Genesis to Revelation,* a comprehensive, verse-by-verse, book-by-book study of the Bible, will strengthen your understanding and appreciation of the Scripture. Order your copy today from *cokesbury.com.*

How You Sleep Affects Your Health

As you drift off to sleep, how does your nightly position affect your health? Whether you prefer stomach, back, side, or curled into a fetal position, the way you snuggle into the pillow may affect your breathing patterns, neck and back pain, and circulation. A less-serious effect, but one most people would probably like to avoid, is an increase in facial wrinkles.

Sleeping Position Pros and Cons

Here are some of the pros and cons of go-to nightly postures, according to the National Sleep Foundation.

1) Back: Lying on your back and assuming a neutral body position typically results in the least amount of strain on your head, neck, and spine. But studies show links between back-sleepers and snoring, so if this is something you are prone to, try flipping to your side. Also, sleeping on your back is not a good choice if you have sleep apnea, because your tongue can fall back, narrowing the airway.

2) Side: Side-sleeping, which is the most common position for adults, helps to open our airways to allow for steady airflow to the lungs. Researchers have found resting on the side may boost brain health, at least when monitoring the sleeping patterns of laboratory animals, but a separate study showed the potential for increased wrinkles in side-sleepers.

3) Fetal position: The fetal position helps improve circulation and is a good bet for people who tend to snore. Be sure not to curl too tightly as you drift off, however, as it may cause difficulty breathing.

4) Stomach: Sleeping on your stomach may make breathing regularly a challenge because airway passages could be compromised. Others may experience neck pain or tingling in joints and muscles due to poor circulation, which is a common challenge for people with diabetes. To help avoid putting pressure on the spine, tuck a pillow under your pelvis to keep a neutral lumbar position. One other negative: enhanced wrinkles may be a side effect of stomach slumber.

While changing your default sleeping position is no easy task, you can help the process by supporting your head and legs with pillows designed for your ideal position.

"Regardless of your go-to sleep position, getting adequate rest is important to all aspects of your health," said Dr. James Metcalf, a medical director with UnitedHealthcare Medicare & Retirement. "Hours of slumber enable our bodies and minds to recharge. Talk with your doctor if you're having trouble getting a good night's sleep."

Source: Brandpoint

Psalm 13:6

Yes, I will **SING to the LORD** *because he has been* **GOOD to ME.**

Respond

BY SUE MINK

S UE MINK, a graduate of Wesley Theological Seminary and Carnegie-Mellon University, has her home near Charlottesville, Virginia, but she's often not there! With the flexibility of working online, she and her husband, Allan, live in other cities around the world for three-month time blocks twice a year. In the past few years, they've lived in Florence, Italy; York, England; Krakow, Poland; Bocas del Toro, Panama; Barcelona, Spain; and Taipei, Taiwan; with many more places planned to visit.

Along with traveling and learning the cultures of her temporary homes, her interests include art, weaving, scuba diving, and learning to cook world cuisines. Sue and her husband have two adult children, Jessica and Rob, and one grandson. She's been writing for Cokesbury for over a decade and loves studying and researching God's Word.

Unless otherwise noted, all Bible background information comes from *The New Interpreter's Bible*, *The New Interpreter's Study Bible*, *The New Interpreter's Dictionary of the Bible*, or *The CEB Study Bible*.

FORGIVENESS

"Holding onto anger is like drinking poison and expecting the other person to die." Perhaps you have heard that expression. If anger is the poison, then forgiveness is the antidote. Anger and true forgiveness cannot coexist. One wipes out the other.

But forgiveness isn't a quick drink or swallowing a pill. Forgiveness takes some work. It is a process. We sometimes have this mistaken perception that forgiveness is a one-moment decision, or even that over time forgiveness will just wash over us. Or we think that our offering of forgiveness is contingent on someone wanting to be forgiven. If that person says the right thing or does something to make amends, then we can forgive that person.

Except that is not how forgiveness works at all. Sometimes those things do contribute to our ability to forgive, but forgiveness has more to do with the transformation of our own hearts than the actions of anyone else. It is not dependent on the work others do, but instead is dependent on the work God does on us and what we are willing to receive from God.

Joseph's story is a profound narrative of the power of forgiveness. Joseph has every reason to be bitter and angry. Yet, what if he had held on to that anger? How would his story have changed? If he had been surly, would he have been sold to Potiphar or marked to a much lower bidder? If he had been sulking and furious, would he have willingly offered to interpret the other two prisoners' dreams or even been offered the opportunity to attend to them? Would his resentment have kept him from sharing an interpretation generously with Pharaoh? And could his anger have kept him from saving his family, and the whole family of God, in the midst of a famine?

Yet instead, along the way, Joseph found ways to step into the transformative love of God. We can do the same, but only if we open to it. When we do, not only are we transformed, the people and circumstances around us are too.

—Michelle J. Morris

Monday | Psalm 37:1-15

Revenge is human, but this psalm tells us that revenge is not our job. It's our job to patiently trust in God's righteousness, continuing to follow God's Word. By practicing grace in our own lives, we develop peace, even when the world seems out to get us. *Lord, help me to trust in your justice when the world is unjust.*

Tuesday | Genesis 37:1-11

Joseph knew he was favored by both his father and by God, but instead of humbly realizing the responsibilities of power, Joseph broadcast his position before he had even earned it. The resentment this caused tore apart his family and brought his father years of grief. *Lord, help me to accept your blessings with humility.*

Wednesday | Genesis 37:12-22

In the ancient Near East, dreams were understood to be messages from God. Yet, Joseph's brothers believed they could change the prophecy by killing Joseph. They did not understand that while God's plans can be changed by human action, they cannot be stopped. *Lord, remind me of your victories when it seems your way has been thwarted.*

Thursday | Genesis 37:23-30

Reuben tried to save Joseph, but he was not brave enough to stand up to his brothers. Judah saved Joseph, but it was by selling him to slave traders. It is a true act of bravery to counteract sin. Both brothers had a part in protecting Joseph's life, but both were too frightened to prevent their brothers' crimes. *Lord, give me the courage to stand up to those I love when they do wrong.*

Friday | Psalm 31:9-13

This psalm tells us that life can be devastatingly difficult. This particular passage is often shared with those suffering the worst of experiences, such as a painful or terminal illness. The writers of the psalms were no strangers to pain and hardship. Yet, the hope and comfort of God is always available to those who call on God. *Oh, God, comfort me in my distress!*

Saturday | Genesis 37:31-36

Joseph's beautiful coat, once a symbol of love, was turned into a means of deceit. Even after seeing their father's overwhelming grief, the brothers still hid the truth from him, allowing him to mourn for years. The love they wanted so badly was tainted by the lies they told to gain it. *Lord, give me the courage to confess my sins to those I have wronged.*

Sunday | Deuteronomy 33:13-17

Before Moses' death, he blessed each of the tribes of Israel. This is the blessing of the tribe of Joseph. Besides blessings of abundant food and military strength, Moses noted that the one who lives on Sinai (God) will always favor him, and that he is the prince among all his brothers. Through all Joseph's trials, God's favor never left him. *Lord, may I always trust in your love for me.*

{ **Key Verses:** "What do we gain if we kill our brother and hide his blood? Come on, let's sell him to the Ishmaelites. Let's not harm him because he's our brother; he's family." (Genesis 37:26-27) }

JOSEPH AND HIS BROTHERS

Lesson: Genesis 37:5-28 • **Background:** Genesis 37:1-36

Think back on times when your life changed dramatically from a coincidental event. Maybe that person you met by chance became your spouse. Perhaps that conversation you had with a stranger changed your outlook on something. That comment by a coworker possibly transformed your career. When you consider the ways your life may have been different but for a chance event, everything can seem quite precarious! But those events only affected your life. What if what happened to you affected a nation? the entire world?

When Abraham was called by God, God told him that he would be the father of nations and his descendants would be the hope of the world. This promise was passed on to his son, Isaac, and from there, to his grandson, Jacob. Much of the Book of Genesis is the story of how that hope moved through those generations. But during that time, God's promise seemed terrifyingly precarious, resting on just one person at a time in the same small family. The story of Joseph tells us how God broadened that family of hope into a nation of hope, even though during Joseph's lifetime, the line of the covenant seemed to get even more precarious!

One reason for all that tension is that Genesis is also a book about dysfunctional families. Abraham sent away his first son, Ishmael, and his son's mother, Hagar, at his wife Sarah's insistence. Jacob used deceit and trickery to steal the promise from his favored brother, Esau. And in this story, Jacob had thirteen sons, but it was the second youngest—in this passage still an arrogant and spoiled boy named Joseph, hated by his older brothers—who was the one to ensure that the family of the covenant survived and grew. Maybe that's why Genesis is so timeless; we can certainly relate. Families still deal with arrogance, jealousy, favoritism, and guilt today.

Joseph was the oldest of Jacob's beloved wife Rachel, well-loved because of how long Rachel had waited for a child of her own. Jacob sent Joseph out to check up on his brothers when Joseph was seventeen, a task he enjoyed just a little too much. He was a tattletale, and his criticisms stung even more because of the coat his father had made for him. Translations differ on its description. It could have been long-sleeved, richly embroidered, or as tradition says, very colorful. Whatever it was, it was a coat designed for royalty, and a coat that broadcast Joseph as his father's unequivocal favorite.

As if that wasn't enough, Joseph dreamed some dreams about his family that a prudent person would have kept to themselves. Even his father questioned why he talked about them. At that time, dreams were understood to be a gift or insight from God, which Joseph's dreams later proved to be. In the first dream, his brothers' sheaves of wheat bowed down to his. This was a foreshadowing of the famine which would cause his brothers to come to him in Egypt in need. In the second dream, the sun and moon (representing his father and mother) and eleven stars (representing his older brothers) all bowed down to him. Clearly, these were dreams about position and power. Some commentators say that the first dream showed Joseph would rule over his brothers in earthly, physical matters, and that the second dream meant he was placed over them in the realm of heaven. Traditionally, older brothers had more authority simply because of their age, but Jacob's favoritism and Joseph's dreams were a threat to that. If they wanted to claim the position their birthright gave them, they had to do something about Joseph.

Jacob favored Joseph, and despite all that Joseph suffered, God clearly favored Joseph too. He was the one with the vision who saved his family, the family that became the Hebrew nation. And so while we can read this story simply as brothers trying to protect their own status and power, it can also be read as a story that is repeated over and over in the Scriptures. Like David who became king, like Gideon who became a military hero, and like a tiny baby born to poor teenaged Jewish parents and laid in a manger, it's the story of how the least likely was able to change the power dynamics of the known world. The dreamer of dreams was and always is a threat to present order. And like all the other unlikely dreamers, if Joseph's visions of power could be believed, then the only thing for the brothers to do to save their own position was to eliminate him.

And so the next time Jacob sent Joseph out to check up on his brothers, they made a plan. They would capture Joseph and kill him, putting an end to his dreams. Ironically, his oldest brother, Reuben, the one with the most to lose from Joseph, argued for his life. He persuaded the other brothers to put him into a dry well, planning to rescue him later. But he left the scene, and another brother, Judah, convinced the rest to sell Joseph to traveling traders. Judah saved Joseph's life at the price of Joseph being enslaved in a foreign country. The slave business between Canaan and Egypt was bustling at the time, and Joseph's slave price, twenty shekels of silver, was a good price for a young man. Judah avoided the guilt of fratricide and got paid well besides.

Imagine how Joseph felt. Sitting in that dry well, helpless, he must have heard his brothers arguing about killing him. Did he get a strong dose of humility as he realized how his behavior had caused his brothers to hate him? Did he feel betrayed? He may have resigned himself to this being the end of his story. Yet, if he believed in his dreams, he knew God had chosen him for greatness. Why would God show him that he was to become a powerful leader if he was to die in a pit by the hands of his brothers? God's plans cannot be thwarted, but they certainly can be impacted by human actions: if Joseph was to become the carrier of the promise, his brothers' actions caused a major detour! While God's plans cannot be thwarted, God's plans also aren't a fortune-teller's description of the future. We must work with God to see God's plans come to fruition. As we continue to read Joseph's story, we find that one of the most important tensions throughout the entire saga of Joseph is the balance between human deeds and the will of God.

After selling him, his brothers tore and bloodied his beautiful coat, a symbol of his father's affection. Given to his son in love, his other sons returned it to Jacob in deceit as proof of Joseph's death. Jacob was inconsolable. He told his family he would mourn for Joseph for the rest of his life, and even his afterlife. Perhaps he had known Joseph was the one who had been holding God's promise for the future of his people, and that's why he was so favored. Perhaps that is why Jacob gave him a coat meant for royalty. If so, Jacob was not only mourning the death of his son, but the death of the promise to his people. After three generations, it seemed as though the covenant lay torn and stained with blood, like the beautiful coat. How would God interact with his people if the favored son, the covenant-bearer, had died?

However, we know that all hope was not gone. Joseph was not dead, but alive. He was a slave in Egypt, but he had been sold to a high official where he would most likely be treated well. Just as God had protected him in the pit through the actions of two of his brothers, he was now protected in Egypt. The story of the covenant may have been hanging by a thread, but it was not over.

Maturing in Faith

"Dare to dream!" read a poster in a school where I once taught. The students were told that dreaming was about believing in themselves and what they could achieve. But dreams in Scripture are about believing in God and what God can achieve. Jesus Christ told his followers about the dream of the kingdom of heaven: a promise of a healed, whole world that will come to earth with his return. Dr. Martin Luther King repeated Scripture's dream of a world based on justice and equality. Dreams like that remake society, and so that kind of dream can often be threatening. The dreams given to us by God change the dynamics of our world.

Joseph's brothers were caught in that change. They saw themselves as the losers in the deal, and so their answer was to destroy the dream. They tried, and for a while, they thought they succeeded. But while their goal was to gain the love of their father, instead Jacob became consumed by grief, broken by their deceit. Their attempt to end God's dream ended their own dreams too.

Sometimes the pathways of God's dreams are changed by the actions of people, but God's dreams are never defeated. Jacob's dysfunctional family still was the stuff of God's plan—the nation of Israel rose up in a foreign country instead. And while Jacob's sons believed they had to defend their places in the story, each one of them founded one of the tribes of Israel. They were not irrelevant but integral to their own branch of the family tree, to God's dream of a nation of people.

While it is daring to believe in your dreams, it is even more daring to believe in the dreams of God. They are radical and often disruptive, but they have a place for every one of us who dares to join in the vision of a world where God's dreams can one day become reality.

Monday | Psalm 1:1-6

Godly people do not let themselves be influenced by those without integrity. Instead, they draw strength from the word and presence of God. Like a well-watered tree, they grow strong and their faith prospers. Joseph refused to betray Potiphar and the teachings of the Lord. Even though he was punished for it, God did not abandon him. *Oh, Lord, may my way be the way of righteousness.*

Tuesday | Genesis 39:1-6a

Those who live by the Word of God positively affect those around them. Even though Potiphar did not worship the Lord, he was astute enough to see that Joseph's presence blessed his home. God's care for Joseph translated into care for Potiphar and his home. God's work through one righteous person affected many. *Oh, Lord, may my obedience to you result in blessings for others.*

Wednesday | Genesis 39:6b-20a

Even righteous people are vulnerable to the sins of others, but that does not mean God has abandoned them. Joseph refused the advances of Potiphar's wife, remaining faithful to both God and Potiphar. God never left him and continued to bless him as he was punished for a false accusation. *Lord, strengthen my trust in you when bad things happen to me.*

Thursday | Proverbs 6:20-26

Commandments about morality are not just prohibitions but protections. Wise parents teach their children to be moral, not just to be godly people, but because immoral behavior can destroy others. Actions that disregard the well-being of others can eventually destroy the sinner as well. *Lord, keep me from harming others through my misdeeds.*

Friday | Genesis 39:20b-23

Joseph was wronged by Potiphar's wife, but he did not let her actions change his character. Joseph remained faithful to God, and God remained with Joseph, blessing him with *hesed*, everlasting love. Like Potiphar, the jailer was also blessed because of Joseph's faithfulness. *Lord, guard my faithfulness to you in all circumstances.*

Saturday | Genesis 40:1-15, 23

Joseph's interpretation of the dreams of Pharaoh's officers demonstrated that God was with him, even in the dungeon. The wine steward was Joseph's hope for release, but he forgot him, leaving him in jail for two more years. Nevertheless, the seed was planted, and when Pharaoh needed an interpreter, the wine steward finally remembered Joseph. *Lord, give me patience when waiting for your blessings.*

Sunday | Genesis 40:16-22

Joseph's interpretation of the baker's dream was bad news for the baker, but Joseph still told him the insight he received from God. It must have been difficult for Joseph to reveal that the baker would soon die in shame, but he was honest with the interpretation. Insights we receive from God are not always easy. *Lord, help me accept your difficult teachings.*

{ **Key Verses:** While he was in jail, the LORD was with Joseph and remained loyal to him. He caused the jail's commander to think highly of Joseph. (Genesis 39:20-21) }

JOSEPH IN POTIPHAR'S HOUSE

Lesson: Genesis 39:1-21 • **Background:** Genesis 39:1–40:23

One of the themes all throughout Scripture is the tension caused when a person of God suffers. Fully one-third of the Psalms are cries of lament. In them, the psalmist loves God but questions God's care in the midst of difficulty. If God is a God of *hesed*, of steadfast love, how can a believer reconcile horrible things that happen in their lives? Why would God allow these things to happen to God's beloved people?

This is an important subtext to the story of Joseph too. Joseph was the one chosen by God to ensure the survival of the covenant. One would think that God would take good care of him. And God did! God made sure that Potiphar prospered when Joseph ran his household. Later, the jailer recognized Joseph's abilities and allowed him to run the jail. People respected him and he was successful, despite being a slave in a foreign land. It is clear from the text that God was at work for Joseph, and he had not been abandoned, despite being outside of both the family and the land of promise. Joseph's story reminds us that even having God's blessing doesn't protect us from the bad actions of others.

The wife of Potiphar, Joseph's owner, set out to seduce Joseph. (She is named Zuleika in the Hebrew midrash, which is an ancient Judaic commentary.) Although he refused her advances numerous times, she was persistent, and perhaps a little upset to be turned down by a slave. Joseph told her that sleeping with her would not only be disloyal to Potiphar, but to God. God had made sure he would prosper, and by committing the sin of adultery, he would be disobedient to them both. But Zuleika was determined. She lied and betrayed him, using his cloak as evidence against him, just as his brothers had used his beautiful coat of many colors as evidence when they lied about Joseph to his father.

God is all-powerful, but things don't always go God's way in the world. Even though God was with Joseph, Joseph, like all of us, was vulnerable to those who would do him harm. God works in a world full of human error, mistakes, and disobedience. Although it saddens God and it is not ever God's will that we sin, if God did not allow us to sin, we would be little more than puppets, blindly following a scripted path. This means that even the most righteous sometimes suffer, and God's beloved people must deal with the consequences of other people's sins as well as their own. Joseph suffered for the sin of Zuleika, Potiphar's wife. Once more, he was betrayed and sent to the pit, this time a jailer's dungeon.

Many of us know someone who has been godly and faithful, but unjustly accused or suffered because of the sins of someone else. Maybe it has even happened to you. When I was in seminary, a classmate of mine was arrested and imprisoned when his young son discovered some cash in a bag and brought it to him. The money was a drop for a criminal extortion which the police had staked out and were watching. It was wrongly supposed that he was part of the plot. It took months for his name to be cleared and for him to be released. Yet through it, he never doubted God was with him. Like Joseph, his faith and knowledge of God's presence comforted him and gave him the strength to deal with his difficulties.

God's continuing presence enabled Joseph to capture the trust of the jailer, just as Potiphar had trusted him. After he had risen to a level of importance in the jail, the pharaoh imprisoned two of his officers: his baker and his chief cupbearer. The cupbearer's job was to taste the king's wine to make sure it was not poisoned. Cupbearers were usually also trusted advisors to the pharaoh. The baker was responsible for the bread served in the household. Commentators have suggested that because both of their duties involved food, perhaps the reason they were imprisoned was an attempted poisoning.

Both officers had disturbing dreams and were concerned about their meanings. In ancient Egypt, dream interpretation was considered an art. Dream interpreters were kept on staff for the pharaoh, and "dream books" still survive from that period which describe the meaning of dreams. People considered dreams so important that they would go to special chambers to sleep in hopes of an insightful dream. While the Hebrews didn't hold high regard for professional dream interpreters, they did believe some dreams were sent by God, and that God could give someone insight through their dreams. Because Joseph knew that God was present with him, he believed he could accurately interpret the officer's dreams. In fact, he told them that only God can interpret dreams. Since God was with him, and presumably not with the professional Egyptian dream interpreters, his analysis would be the correct one.

The dreams were clearly meant to be interpreted as a pair. Both had three items, and both involved the officers' professions. The cupbearer's dream showed him resuming his duties. Joseph assured him that was the meaning. The three vines in his dream signified three days, and after then, he would make wine and present it to the king as he had before. The baker's dream was more ominous. Birds ate the bread he had made for the pharaoh from three baskets balanced on his head, just as they would eat the baker's flesh after his execution in three days. In both interpretations, Joseph used the phrase "lift your head." In the cupbearer's case, his head would be lifted again from shame to restored dignity. In the baker's case, his head would be lifted off his body! For both men, Joseph's interpretations were correct.

Knowing the cupbearer had the ear of the king, Joseph asked him to present his case to the pharaoh and help him get out of jail. But the cupbearer forgot about Joseph once he returned to his position. Again, God's plans were diverted because of human will. Joseph stayed two more years in prison before the cupbearer finally remembered him.

This world is stained with sin. That causes all people to be vulnerable, not only to their own temptation, but to the results of the sins of society, of our communities, and of other individuals. Our own righteousness does not protect us from all the evils in the world. Bad things do happen to good people. Theologians have struggled with this truth for centuries. Does that mean God is not really all that powerful? Or if God has the power to change horrible situations, does that mean God doesn't care, and that God's *hesed*, God's everlasting, all-encompassing love is a lie? The story of Joseph offers another explanation. God shows *hesed* through presence with God's beloved people, even while allowing humanity to make mistakes and go against God's great plan for redemption and salvation. Sometimes God works powerful, recognizable miracles to correct human mistakes, such as when an earthquake released Paul from prison. But many times, God's work is subtle, behind the scenes, and takes time and discernment to understand. Joseph knew that he prospered, not only because of his own abilities but because God was with him. Despite the horrible things that happened to him, he remained faithful and obedient to God. This tension between God's care and human foibles is at the very heart of living to please the Lord in the midst of a broken world.

Maturing in Faith

Last year, I visited the spectacular Plitvice waterfalls in Croatia. The mountains there are full of lakes, and the rivers that run downhill create thousands of waterfalls in a small region. However, because the water is so rich with minerals, the course of the water is constantly changing. As the minerals build up, the water must find a new route down the mountain. The result is ever-shifting paths where many streams make their way through the forest, constantly transforming the landscape.

Such it is with the plans of God. They will always come to pass, just as water must always run downhill. However, God has granted humanity the freedom of choice, even to choose sin. Those choices sometimes block the pathways of God's plans. But like water running downhill, there is always another way. The route may change, but the result will not.

God's great plan is for humanity to experience salvation and for the world to be healed and whole. The Hebrew people were integral to this plan, and so even when Joseph, the keeper of the covenant, was sent as a slave to Egypt, the course of the plan just changed, not the plan itself. We can completely trust that God's plans will come to fruition, just as we can trust that water will always run downhill. The path may change. The end goal will not.

This truth is the intersection of real life and real faith. Real life is full of twists and turns, mistakes, upsets, and barriers. When we think about the effects of sin in the world, both by individuals and by society, it can break our hearts and even our spirit. But real faith tells us that God will always find a way. God's creative action in the world carves new pathways and finds new means to bring about God's blessings. Our God is a God of constant and unstoppable hope.

Monday | Genesis 41:1-16

Joseph waited in prison for two years before the cupbearer remembered Joseph. Yet, when called before Pharaoh, the first words out of Joseph's mouth were to give God glory. The pharaoh knew his own weaknesses, and Joseph was not afraid to state that it was God who had the true power. *Lord, give me the courage to give you the glory.*

Tuesday | Genesis 41:17-32

We may not usually think of dreams as the means to understand God's ways today. In ancient Egypt, dreams were studied and believed in. God used the belief system of the Egyptians for God's own revelation and to place Joseph in a position of power. God can use many different means to reach people, even those that may be unfamiliar to us. *Lord, help me to see your work, even in unfamiliar places.*

Wednesday | Genesis 41:33-45

Joseph's faithfulness and trust in God resulted in the pharaoh placing him in a powerful position, which enabled God to use him to further God's plans. It was not a reward but a responsibility. God works to place each one of us where we can do the work of the Lord. *Open my eyes to what you would have me do, where you have placed me.*

Thursday | Genesis 41:46-57

We talk about doing things for God, but how often do we actually follow through? Joseph trusted the knowledge God gave him to collect the grain from the abundant years to help with the lean times. Joseph's obedience alleviated much suffering and ultimately brought his family back together. *Lord, help me to persevere in the work that you've given me to do for you.*

Friday | Genesis 47:27-31

Jacob's dying wish was to be buried with his ancestors back in Hebron. He knew he was an heir to God's promise, and that the land was integral to that promise. It was only when he knew that promise would be honored that he allowed his soul to leave his body. *Lord, keep me faithful to your promises and may my life reflect my dedication to you.*

Saturday | Genesis 49:22-26, 28

Jacob's blessing to Joseph asserts his strength in adversity and his special blessings as the protector of the promise. Joseph remained faithful to God throughout all his difficulties, and God blessed him for it. It is because of God working through Joseph that the story continued. *Lord, strengthen me during my difficulties so that I may remain faithful to you.*

Sunday | Acts 7:9-16

The martyr Stephen told Joseph's story to those who stoned him. Like Joseph, Stephen put his destiny into God's hands. God used them in very different ways, but both men forwarded God's vision for the world by inspiring and enabling others to know the power of God. *Lord, use me so that you may be glorified.*

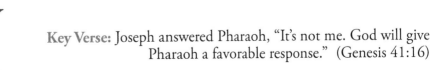

Key Verse: Joseph answered Pharaoh, "It's not me. God will give Pharaoh a favorable response." (Genesis 41:16)

JOSEPH INTERPRETS PHARAOH'S DREAM

Lesson: Genesis 41:1-16, 25-32 • **Background:** Genesis 41:1-57

Egypt is a desert whose only source of water is the Nile River. In ancient times, the Nile flooded every June, spreading out across the huge Nile delta region. The water stayed until late September or early October, creating rich soil from the minerals washed from the mountains in the south. Immediately, the farmers in ancient Egypt would plant their crops, harvesting them in the spring before the Nile flooded again. The entire livelihood of Egypt was based on the flooding of the Nile. Too much water, and the towns were destroyed. Not enough, and the land wouldn't be watered enough for crops and there would be famine.

The pharaoh had the status of a deity. The Egyptian religion taught that the pharaoh controlled the Nile and the amount of flooding each year. The pharaoh could demand worship from the people because they believed he controlled their only source of food, but it also tied the fate of the Pharaoh very closely to the rise and fall of the Nile's flood waters. A bad year for the Nile could be disastrous for the pharaoh. This is why the pharaoh in this Scripture passage was so concerned about his dreams. If the flooding should fail, then not only would his people starve, but he would be discredited as the god of the Nile. The pharaoh was desperate to find out the meaning of his dreams, and so after his dream interpreters failed, he was ready to listen to even a jailed Hebrew. Joseph was called out of prison and prepared to meet the most powerful man in Egypt. His beard was cut off to make him appear more like a clean-shaven Egyptian, and he was given a new cloak. Twice before his cloaks were taken from him when things went wrong. Once his beautiful cloak of many colors was taken by his brothers, and he was sold into slavery. The second time, Potiphar's wife stole his cloak and used it to betray him, resulting in his imprisonment. This time, he was given a cloak. Things were looking up.

The pharaoh's dreams came in pairs, like all the other dreams in the Joseph narrative. In the first dream, fat and healthy cows were devoured by ugly, skinny cows. In the second, fat grains of wheat were eaten up by withered, dry grains. Both dreams meant the same thing. There would be seven years of plenty, followed by seven years of famine. The pharaoh immediately accepted Joseph's interpretation and was grateful for his insight. An alert reader, however, should pay attention to Joseph's exact words. He was very careful to say that the dreams foretold what God would do. God was in control of the Nile and the flooding. Joseph was bold enough to tell the pharaoh, the Egyptian "deity" who people believed controlled the Nile floodwaters, that it was not the pharaoh but the Lord God who was in charge of the waters. It was because God said so that it would be so.

I think it would be a terrifying thing to be responsible for something you actually had no control over. The pharaoh must have known he couldn't control the Nile waters. And so when Joseph was able to tell him what would happen for the next fourteen years, it must have come as a relief to him. Joseph suggested he put a person in place to build granaries to store excess grain during the prosperous years to have food during the lean ones. The pharaoh could put this impossible situation into the hands of someone else. He immediately named Joseph to the position. Commentators have written how remarkable it was that the pharaoh accepted Joseph's analysis without question, immediately relinquishing his control over Egypt's rule. But the pharaoh never actually had control. He could finally rest knowing it was God who controlled the waters, and that Joseph would take responsibility for feeding his people.

Joseph became highly respected. He was given a chariot and heralded as he traveled. The pharaoh gave him an Egyptian name, *Zaphenath-paneah,* which means "God Speaks and Lives." His wife was from nobility. This story of the rapid rise of a slave might seem a bit unbelievable, but there is historical evidence that the events recounted here were not impossible. Rulers in ancient Egypt had recognized talent before, and slaves from that time period were sometimes promoted into high positions. There is also evidence of granaries from that time period. The Nile was unreliable, and it makes sense that they would save surplus grain from abundant crops.

Joseph and his wife had two sons and their names reflected the changes God had made in Joseph's life. The first son was named *Manasseh,* which means "making to forget." Joseph was able to put the betrayal of his family behind him. The second son he named *Ephraim,* which was Hebrew for "fruitful." Here, in this new land, God made Joseph affluent and powerful. Jacob's beloved son, Joseph, had become a crucial Egyptian official. He had forgotten his painful past and was celebrating his present and future.

It's important to remember, however, that the story does not end here. God didn't bless Joseph and make him prosper because he was a favorite son and that's what God does for his favorites. Instead, God had placed Joseph in a position of power and authority so God could use him to help realize God's plans. God is less interested in our personal comfort and glory and more interested in the forward motion of God's vision for the world. Those who follow and obey God allow themselves to be used by God. God placed Joseph in a position where he could facilitate God's plans.

God opened both Joseph and Pharaoh's eyes to an upcoming crisis, but Joseph used his own intellect and resources to find a solution. Again, this story tells us about the interaction between God and humanity. Before in Joseph's saga, when people disobeyed God, God found another way to forward God's plan for Joseph and God's vision. But here, a faithful man was given knowledge by God, and working with that knowledge, he saved thousands from starvation. God works through and with those who listen and obey God. God does not expect people to be passive and simply accept the ways of the world. Instead, we are given talents and abilities to work with God and to better the world. In this example, God used a wise leader to avert economic disaster. God gave Joseph important knowledge of the upcoming famine, but because of insightful human organization and preparation, the impact of the famine was minimized.

God and humanity interact in a dance of both tension and obedience. The purposes of God are tied to concrete actions by humans. When people disobey or thwart God's plans, God must redirect God's action to find other ways. But when people understand God's revelations and join in God's plans, their creative action helps to forward God's vision. This complex interaction between God and human beings is full of twists and turns, just like the story of Joseph. But because of God's great *hesed,* God's everlasting and eternal love for all of us, the end goal is God's gift of grace and salvation for humanity. If our disobedience puts barriers in the way of God's plans for us, then God finds another way. But when faithful and obedient people hear and respond to God's call, the vision of God is furthered and salvation is that much closer for all.

Maturing in Faith

When I was in Taiwan, I sometimes watched the people pray in the temples. They practiced a radically different religion than Christianity. They believed deities listened to requests, decided who was blessed, and let their decisions be known by a roll of dice. The deities were there strictly to fill the peoples' needs.

God is not here for our needs. Rather, we are here, where we are, in order to further God's vision and desires in the world. God's job is not to make us happy and to give us things we want. Rather, we are given talents and resources in order to find our joy in serving the Lord.

Joseph was given the ability to interpret dreams by God. God gave Joseph the opportunity to interpret the pharaoh's dreams and placed him in a position of power, wealth, and prestige. This was not a reward from God for Joseph's faithfulness, but a responsibility from God to use what he was given to further God's vision for the world. Like every one of us, he was called to always be a servant of God.

What are your talents and abilities? What positions or resources has God given you? Each one of them are responsibilities to further the kingdom of God. Even if your gifts seem simple and your place in the world is modest, God is able to use every faithful and obedient person to bring God's kingdom closer to earth.

Often when we pray, it's a list of requests for God. Christ told us we can ask for anything in his name, so this in itself is not wrong. But our purpose on earth is to serve the Lord, and our first request should be to hear God's voice in direction for our lives, so we can be effective servants and stewards of God's gifts and grace to us.

Monday | Genesis 42:1-24

Joseph wasn't prepared for seeing his brothers after so many years, yet his brothers never forgot him. They carried guilt and shame for their sin and believed God was punishing them. Joseph cried when he realized their pain, but he wasn't yet ready to forgive them. *Lord, soften my heart toward those who need my forgiveness.*

Tuesday | Genesis 43:1-34

The brothers were frightened to see Joseph again because they had found the money in their grain sacks, but the steward assured them that the treasure in their sacks was the work of God. Even if not placed there by God, God had begun to soften Joseph's heart, enabling him to return the money. *Lord, open me to possibilities of reconciliation.*

Wednesday | Genesis 44:1-17

Joseph enacted an elaborate ruse to get Benjamin back to Egypt and send the other brothers home. Benjamin was Joseph's only full brother, and he alone was innocent in Joseph's betrayal. Joseph wanted to keep Benjamin for himself without revealing himself to the other brothers, causing pain to the rest of his family. *Lord, keep me aware of how my actions may be affecting others.*

Thursday | Genesis 44:18-34

Judah's integrity finally allowed Joseph to forgive. Joseph understood how much his father had grieved after his disappearance and how his father's grief had caused his other brothers to live in guilt and remorse. God used the experience to change all of them and caused them to protect and love one another. *Lord, use my life experiences to teach me love and compassion.*

Friday | Genesis 45:1-15

Joseph was able to put the past behind him because the present had become aligned with God's purposes. All the pain and sin in the family had been used by God to bring healing and life to them all. God used their actions to avert a famine and to reunite the family of promise, weaving their actions into a blessing for them and for the world. *Lord, thank you for creating blessings despite our sinful human actions.*

Saturday | Genesis 45

Joseph's brothers were new men. They could go to their father, admit the truth, but celebrate because God created goodness out of their sin. Jacob, who waited in fear to hear the fate of Benjamin, cried out in joy when he found out that both sons of Rachel were alive. *Lord, may I rejoice in the healing and hope your blessings bring!*

Sunday | Psalm 105:16-23

Joseph's story was not just the story of the healing of a family but a story of rescuing a nation. Because of Joseph's position in Egypt, the Hebrew people didn't starve in the famine. God's blessings extended from the family of promise to the Hebrew people and even on to saving the Egyptians. *Lord, thank you for your grace and care of all your people.*

{ Key Verse: "Now, don't be upset and don't be angry with yourselves that you sold me here. Actually, God sent me before you to save lives." (Genesis 45:5) }

JOSEPH FORGIVES HIS BROTHERS

Lesson: Genesis 45:1-15 • **Background:** Genesis 42:1–45:27

Anyone who has experienced estrangement knows how difficult it is to heal a broken relationship. It takes courage to face possible rejection. It takes forgiveness for past wrongs. It takes the ability to trust again and determination to work through the pain of revisiting past mistakes and affronts. When I read this passage about when Joseph saw his brothers for the first time in many years, I finally see Joseph as a flawed human being. Joseph had been the model of a godly person, but I certainly don't admire how he treated his brothers at first. He played them like a cat with a mouse, using his position of power to return the grief they caused him. He wasn't godly. He acted like a vengeful person who had been terribly wronged.

Some commentators excuse Joseph by saying that he needed to test his brothers to make sure they had truly repented of their actions before he revealed himself. Possibly this was a reason for some of what he did. But I don't think readers should gloss over the difficulties of healing estrangement. It's hard work, and forgiveness doesn't always come easy. Joseph didn't expect to see his brothers the first time. He was unprepared for all the emotions that seeing them would stir up in him. Despite what he had named his son (*Manasseh,* "making to forget"), his actions make it clear that he didn't really forget what his brothers had done to him. It didn't seem as though he wanted to renew the relationship with his brothers or even his father. His only passion was for his brother, Benjamin, the only other son of his mother. It was just because of Benjamin that he even interacted with his brothers. His goal was to get Benjamin to Egypt and to figure out a way that he alone would stay there with him.

And so this series of "tests" were tests both of his brothers and of Joseph himself. The brothers had to confront what they had done to Joseph and to deal with the guilt. They had not forgotten. They believed they were still being punished by God for their sin against Joseph when Joseph put them in prison and accused them of being spies. When Joseph let them all go, but Simeon, the brothers continued to argue among themselves about what they had done to Joseph. It was front and foremost on their minds, and they were living with the guilt every day. They also were extremely protective of Benjamin, knowing he was the only son left of Rachel and was their father's favorite, as Joseph had been. They would not hurt their father so grievously again.

But Joseph had to decide that he wanted a relationship with his brothers and to learn how to forgive them. Joseph wept three times in this story, each one as he became more and more aware of his brothers' sorrow and guilt over what they had done to him. Each time, he was re-evaluating his relationship with them. Each time, he was confronting his ability to forgive. Finally, Judah's pleas broke his heart and he told them who he was. The entire family was brought to a new moment. Joseph was able to put the past behind him for real. The brothers were able to accept forgiveness and live without the guilt that had been haunting them for years. Joseph and his brothers both did the hard work of reconciliation.

But it was also God's work and God's purpose, made concrete in human history. Joseph told his brothers that God had orchestrated the situation to bring them together and to guide them to healing and reconciliation. It was not by the grace of Joseph that the family was reunited. Joseph struggled mightily with forgiveness. In the moment of revelation, he realized God had worked through human events to bring them to the place of healing and a place of plenty. It was a new beginning for all of them, crafted by God to heal the human events that caused their painful circumstances.

Human beings have choice. The world is full of human sinfulness that corrupts the holiness of creation. People hurt one another, families split apart, and we all experience suffering caused by selfishness, fear, greed, and coldheartedness. But God continues to be at work, not only despite human beings, but through human beings. God used even the pain of Joseph's story to reestablish reconciliation and life for those who would have walked away from one another in the midst of both physical and emotional famine. God's saving work uses humanity, just as humanity is guided by God's grace and goodness. As human beings, we are free to do what we will, but every one of our actions can be used by God to further God's will in the world.

Every day God works through human actions, both good and bad. Lou Williams was a basketball player for the Philadelphia 76ers. When he was off the court, he remembered his roots in the community and handed out coats to the homeless and supported a camp for children. One Christmas Eve, he was stopped in his car at a traffic light and a man knocked on his window, pointing a gun at him. When he rolled down the window, the man recognized him and lowered the gun. "I can't do this," he said, "not to you. You do so much for the community." He went on to explain that he had just gotten out of jail, he was homeless and hungry, and felt he had no other option but to continue in crime. "Get in the car," Lou told him. He took him to a nearby McDonald's where they ate a meal together and talked for hours. Lou Williams helped him get on his feet again. A desperate man made a terrible choice in attempting a robbery, but God used the situation for healing and renewal.

God has a plan for the world and for our salvation. The final culmination of God's plan, the kingdom of heaven come to earth when Jesus Christ returns, is a promise we can believe with absolute certainty. God's plan is one of ultimate, complete healing and reconciliation. But along the way, there are what author Jonathan Kozol calls "ordinary resurrections"—small miracles of healing, of renewal, and of grace that right the pathway of humanity in countless ways. God uses each one of us to be players in these ordinary resurrections, weaving us into God's life-giving story. God's activities are factors in every event on earth, even when we don't recognize God's presence.

Joseph sent his brothers to bring his father to Egypt so the entire family could live together and survive the famine. Jacob responded first in disbelief and then with great joy. His son who had been lost was found! Even with a dozen other sons, he had spent years grieving for Joseph, and he knew then the promise from God that his family was to carry was not ended. Joseph was the embodiment of the promise carried from Abraham, and that promise was still alive! Jacob had spent his life pursuing and then guarding the promise. He walked with a limp, the result of wrestling with God when he reached for his place in the covenant. To know Joseph was alive was to know the covenant was still alive, too, and that God had not abandoned his family. Joseph's story is not just the tale of how a family was fed during a famine, but a story of reconciliation, of hope, and of how God's great design works within human history for our salvation.

Maturing in Faith

This story of Joseph is about being bold for God. It's about forgiveness and letting go of anger. But most importantly, it's about hope. It taught me there is an ultimate power in this world that, despite our mistakes and faults, relentlessly works for our good.

We control our own lives, and in this world of sin, that can be pretty terrifying. Human beings, even godly people like Joseph, can make terrible choices. But God is intimately involved in the world, molding and crafting events to ultimately work toward God's own vision. The thrust of God's action, always weaving its way through earthly events, is for the good of humankind. God's active work in the world enhances and respects our freedom, while giving us an opportunity to join together with God while God heals and reconciles.

So, this means that despite our mistakes and despite the mistakes of others, we can have confidence that the ultimate outcome for humanity will be guided by the all-loving, ever-gracious Lord. Terrible things may happen because people do terrible things. But that will never be the end of the story. God can enable and inspire us to do God's will, changing human hearts in the process. God can also use human actions, both good and bad. We are always part of God's plans.

And so, we can live in hope, despite the pain and hopelessness we sometimes see in the world. All that can be turned around by the Lord, and we have been promised that this is exactly what will happen forever when Jesus Christ returns. While we wait for that wonderful day, we struggle along in faith, seeking to obey and be faithful, but also being confident of God's mercy, forgiveness, and even ability to use our mistakes for God's glory. We don't need to fear. God is forever on our side.

SCRIPTURE

The legal expert asked Jesus what he needed to do to inherit eternal life, and Jesus asked the expert what the Scriptures tell him to do. "You must love the Lord your God with all your heart, with all your being, with all your strength, and with all your mind, and love your neighbor as yourself." So, Jesus tells the man to do that. But then the legal expert asks, "And who is my neighbor?" So, Jesus tells him the story of the good Samaritan who rescues the man who had been beaten and left for dead on the side of the road. When Jesus asks the expert who has been the neighbor, the man points to the Samaritan. Then Jesus tells the expert, "Go and do likewise." (See Luke 10:25-37.)

This story not only teaches us that loving our neighbor is central to our faith, it also models for us another way of growing in our faith: studying and applying Scripture. Now, for the legal expert and Jesus in this moment, the Scriptures were made of books from what we call the Old Testament. The New Testament, of course, didn't exist for Jesus and the expert at the time the story is set. Still, they are showing us first that it is important to know Scripture. When the expert asks Jesus what is the key to eternal life, Jesus points the man to the Scriptures. The key is there. Thus, studying Scripture is central for understanding that journey. The Articles of Religion of the Methodist Church tell us that Scripture contains all things necessary for salvation. It appears Jesus agrees with us!

But Jesus and the expert do not stop there. They dig deeper. If salvation comes from loving God and neighbor, then who is my neighbor? Then Jesus shares a story to help illuminate that. Finally, Jesus tells the man to go and do just like the Samaritan. It is not enough to know the stories. The stories must then also be put to action. The study of Scripture is key to our faith and salvation, but if we do not let it transform us and our world, we have missed the point. Both must go hand-in-hand.

—Michelle J. Morris

Monday | Psalm 118:19-29

Righteous people are not perfect. Instead, they are people who know they are God's beloved and who strive to live within God's commands, thankful for the new life God has offered. It is not only our responsibility but our great joy to praise God as we enter into God's gates, the place of belonging. *Oh, Lord, you are good! Your steadfast love endures forever!*

Tuesday | Exodus 20:13-17

Six of the Ten Commandments deal with our relationship with our neighbors. They represent the most basic behaviors of righteousness, which are respect and dignity to others. While our relationship to God is foremost, God is deeply concerned with how we live in community. *Lord, may my interactions with my neighbors reflect your love for them.*

Wednesday | Exodus 22:5-15

While these specific rules don't apply to modern society, the reasoning behind them is still true. God is concerned about fairness and justice. Neighbors should not take advantage of one another and should provide restitution for damages. While this is true for communities, it is also true on a global scale. We are responsible when our actions hurt others. *Lord, open my eyes to the ways my actions may damage others.*

Thursday | Proverbs 3:27-30

God expects us to treat one another with integrity. Honesty and fairness are crucial to being a good neighbor. In order for people to flourish together in peace as God intends, we need to be trustworthy and never take advantage of one another. *Lord, guide me in being a good neighbor to all.*

Friday | Proverbs 6:1-5

Rash promises or commitments change relationships. People of integrity must honor their commitments, but if the agreement is foolish, until the situation is resolved, relationships can often become strained. Take care when you make a promise to another, so there is no regret or resentment. *Lord, guide me when I make promises to others.*

Saturday | Proverbs 14:20-22

Moral character, rather than wealth, is a person's most important attribute. It may be more prestigious to be friendly with the wealthy, but economics don't always coincide with one's ethics. Being friends with the poor is a way of pleasing the Lord because God commands us to be just and merciful. *Lord, guide me in kindness to all your people.*

Sunday | Proverbs 25:20-23

Anger and revenge only breed more animosity. The only way to break the cycle is with compassion and love. God gives us the difficult command to treat our enemies as friends, giving them food and water when they are hungry and thirsty. Seeing one another as fellow human beings is the first step in healing relationships. *Lord, strengthen my resolve to be merciful to those who have hurt me.*

> **Key Verse:** Don't say to your neighbor, "Go and come back; I'll give it to you tomorrow," when you have it. (Proverbs 3:28)

PROVERBS ABOUT BEING A NEIGHBOR

Lesson: Proverbs 3:27-30; 6:1-5; 25:20-23 • **Background:** Proverbs 3:27-30; 6:1-5; 14:20-22; 25:20-23

Some years ago, my friend Steve Jennings was leading a youth group in a northern Virginia church. He told the teens about God's command to love your neighbor, and the teens questioned him. "People say that all the time," they responded. "What does it really look like to love your neighbor?" The next week, Steve directed them to pack up some clothing and sandwiches, and they went to downtown Washington, DC, to hand them out to people living on the streets. More than thirty years later, Steve still brings teens to the streets of Washington, DC; Richmond, Virginia; Baltimore, Maryland; and other towns to minister to the homeless with food, clothing, and most importantly, friendship. His training emphasizes having a heart to truly listen, a commitment to return to visit the same people on a monthly basis, and to pray for those he and the teens befriend. His organization, Teens Opposing Poverty, has taught young people what it means to be a neighbor and has been the impetus for many people to gain the courage to change their lives and leave the streets. Steve's vision and heart for God has truly taught a great many people, myself included, what it means to love your neighbor.

This isn't just a nice story about a nice man. This is faith in action from a committed Christian dedicated to following the commands of God. The Scriptures are very clear about the importance of loving your neighbor. Jesus himself said that after loving God, loving your neighbor was the most important commandment. But what exactly does it mean to love your neighbor?

It's easy enough to say one should not purposefully hurt another. Proverbs 3:29-30 condemns harming a neighbor, especially by betraying their trust. But Proverbs 3:27-28 goes further to describe a sin of omission, refusing to give others what they deserve when you have the ability to do so. This also sounds simple, but think for a moment about what each person on this earth deserves. The Scriptures deeply value justice, which is equal opportunity for all to prosper. It is key for a working society. Justice within a society means that no person lives under oppression and everyone is given the chance to be able to provide for their basic needs. So, what would make each life

one of justice and opportunity? And what can you do to offer that to others? Maybe you don't have a lot of resources yourself to give to others or can't devote your life to the poor like my friend Steve, and this passage is sympathetic to that. It does not ask that we make ourselves destitute to help others. But it does ask that we examine what we can do, and that we do it. At the very least, we all can offer compassion and affirmation to others. Proverbs 3:27-28 tells us not only to seriously examine what resources we have and how to use them, but not to delay.

This, however, is against human nature. Proverbs 14:20 is a sad commentary about how we truly behave. Those who are rich have plenty of friends, while few are friends to the poor. Quite honestly, we're the most comfortable with people who are similar to ourselves and we don't think will ask anything of us. It's tough to be friends with those others look down on, those who are often in need or are very different culturally or ethnically. But my friend Steve would tell you that a person who was trying to follow the command of loving their neighbor would have many unlikely friendships. They would reach across age, socioeconomic, sexual identity, ethnic and racial barriers to connect with others, not as a "project" but in genuine relationships that enrich all who are involved. We should look to Jesus as the perfect example. He never paid attention to artificial barriers between himself and other people. He interacted with everyone he met with an open heart. From the very poorest beggars to a Roman centurion, Jesus offered access to his heart, just as he does to people from every imaginable background today.

Extending kindness to those who are different from you can be difficult. But even more difficult is being kind to those who are not kind to you. Proverbs 25:21-22 instructs us to make sure that the basic human needs of food and drink are given even to our enemies. Every human being on this planet, no matter how difficult to love, is a creature of God, loved by God. While commentators disagree at the exact meaning of "heap burning coals on their heads" in verse 22, most likely it means that if someone has treated you badly and you respond in kindness, their cruelty to you will come back on them and shame them. It's a rebuke of grace.

This collection of Proverbs addresses other difficulties in relationships with your neighbor. Most talk about looking out for our neighbor's needs, but Proverbs 6:1-5 warns against putting yourself in your neighbor's debt. In ancient Israel, if someone could not pay off what they owed, they could offer themselves as collateral and work off their debt. The sage in Proverbs 6:1-5 warned against this practice. Falling into debt binds a person to another and puts you in their power. This wise man told his children that it was crucial to work as hard as possible to get oneself out of debt as quickly as they could. When money is involved, the relationship with one's neighbor can quickly breed resentment or abuse of the power one has over the other, a situation that perverts the meaning of neighborly love.

In short, loving one's neighbor means seeing every person as a beloved child of God, and so, someone of infinite value. My friend Steve Jennings has taught hundreds of teens to learn the stories of the people who sleep on the streets of Washington, DC, recognizing them as people of worth and treating them with respect. The pastor of my little church found a woman sleeping in her car in the Walmart parking lot, and she was welcomed into the church, taken into a congregant's home, and supported as she got herself back on her feet. There are stories like this all over the world, where people listen to the call of God, see others in distress, and welcome them as their neighbor.

Jesus was once asked, "Who is my neighbor?" In response, he told the parable of the good Samaritan. In the time of Christ, the common opinion of Samaritans was anything but good. Jews condemned them because they had intermarried with the Assyrians during the Babylonian Exile and believed they had perverted the Jewish faith. They would regularly walk miles out of the way to avoid going through Samaritan lands. They would have no business dealings at all with them. Yet, the moral of the story is that the Samaritan is the neighbor. They were to love everyone, not just the people like themselves, not just those they agreed with, and not just those who "belonged" in their lands. *Neighbor* means every person. Everyone. Even those you least suspect. There's no room for discrimination or feelings of superiority.

It takes courage to reach out to someone who is in need, who is not like you, or who has different beliefs. Being a neighbor to all people means allowing yourself to be challenged and maybe even changed by another. But if Jesus said that loving our neighbor is second only to loving God, then we can't really call ourselves disciples if we disobey this crucial command.

Maturing in Faith

Just because you're reading this study, I can surmise you're a person who is dedicated to strengthening your relationship with the Lord. The daily discipline of reading and reflecting on Scripture, prayer, and study builds up our love for God. The Shema (Deuteronomy 6:4-9), known as the greatest commandment, tells us to love God with all our hearts, souls, and strength. But faith is not a strictly personal matter between you and God. Jesus said the second commandment is to love your neighbor as yourself. If your faith is strictly a personal matter, then you're missing half the equation.

How we respond to others is the indicator of how God has changed our hearts. One of the most powerful prayers a person can pray is for God to show them what hurts God's heart, and to make their heart hurt for those things too. One had better be prepared for the answer. There are people everywhere whose circumstances hurt the heart of God. As God's workers in the world, called to love our neighbor, our mission is clear. We are to strive to heal those hurts to the best of our ability, calling on God as our strength and our provider.

God's intent is to have a community who cares for one another, uplifting each of us as we need it. As we give God's love to others, so will we receive it. None of us was meant to go at it alone. God designed the church to love and strengthen one another, but then to reach out in that same love to the greater community, to the state, to the nation, and finally to the entire world. Imagine how the world would look if everyone hurt for the things that hurt God's heart and was dedicated to heal them. Imagine what kind of neighbors we would be to one another.

Monday | Hebrews 6:9-12

The Letter to the Hebrews was written to a congregation who had been strong in the faith and had cared for God's people. These words encouraged them to persist on their path, confident that God had noticed and would continue to support them. We can hear the same encouragement, trusting God will see when we obey God's word to love one another. *Lord, encourage me to love my neighbor.*

Tuesday | Deuteronomy 24:17-22

Gleanings were the leftovers of the harvest. God commands those who have enough to be aware of those who are in need. Who in our society is forced to live on the leftovers? What are the gleanings of today's society that can be left for the needy? *Lord, show me where my surplus is and how I can leave my gleanings for those in need.*

Wednesday | Job 29:11-17

God said that there was no one like Job on the earth, "a man who is honest, who is of absolute integrity" (Job 2:3). Job took responsibility for the vulnerable and needy. His care for others was a source of joy, and he was honored for it. His care was personal and intimate, not just financial but truly meeting their individual needs. *Lord, may I find joy in helping others.*

Thursday | Titus 1:5-9

Those who represent the church have a responsibility to be morally upright and honest. Among the qualities Paul listed were hospitality and loving what is good. Those qualities would welcome others into the fellowship of God, and would teach the members of the church to love as God loves them. *Lord, cultivate the qualities in me that would glorify your church.*

Friday | Leviticus 19:18; Matthew 19:16-22

God loves you with an overwhelming, unquenchable love, but God loves all of creation with that same depth and strength. Loving your neighbor as yourself means to join with God in loving creation and those within it. It's looking beyond yourself to the good of your community and of the world. *Lord, teach me to look at all of creation with your eyes of love.*

Saturday | Ruth 2:3-9

Gleaning was a public statement of need. Ruth worked hard in the fields, and Boaz noticed her and helped her. Often, we simply don't see the needs of others, but Boaz recognized Ruth's circumstances. *Lord, open my eyes to those in need in my community.*

Sunday | Ruth 2:10-16

Boaz allowed Ruth to glean in his field and that was all that was required of him. Yet, he went further to help her by protecting her, allowing her water, feeding her, and giving her extra to glean, even though she was a Moabite. Loving your neighbor doesn't involve only what you have to do, but includes intentional work to meet another's needs. *Lord, show me what my neighbor needs and how I can help to meet those needs.*

Key Verse: Then she got up to glean. Boaz ordered his young men, "Let her glean between the bundles, and don't humiliate her." (Ruth 2:15)

NEIGHBORLY TREATMENT OF AN IMMIGRANT

Lesson: Ruth 2:4-16 • **Background:** Ruth 2:4-16; Leviticus 19:18; Matthew 19:16-22

I taught high school in a neighborhood where there were many immigrants. One of my favorite students was a young woman named Jessica who had been brought into the country illegally as a child. She was a "Dreamer" who applied for the chance to become a citizen in the only country she had ever really known. Jessica was very dedicated to her mother, a domestic worker who struggled to support Jessica and her sister. Jessica herself was a hardworking student and also did whatever odd jobs she could after school to bring in money for her family. When she graduated, she enlisted into the Air Force so that she could be trained in a skill and help her mother even more. After graduation, she sent me a small photo of herself in her uniform, and wrote that she was proud to be contributing to her family and to her adopted country, but worried about the policies affecting Dreamers. In many ways, that young woman was a modern-day Ruth, striving to help those she loved in a country that wasn't sure it wanted her.

Ruth's situation was very much like an illegal immigrant's of today. She was a Moabite, and Deuteronomy 23:3 forbade any Moabite from coming into the assembly of the Lord to the tenth generation. She would not have been welcome in Bethlehem, where she went with Naomi, and was well aware of the hostility she would face. Yet, she loved her mother-in-law and knew that as an elderly woman without any male relatives, Naomi might not survive without her. She braved leaving her homeland, dealing with a unreceptive new culture, and the taunts of those in her new home to care for Naomi. Her first break came when she went to glean in the fields of Boaz, a pillar of the community. Instead of reviling her because she was a foreigner, he honored her dedication to her late husband's mother and arranged so that she might glean more than was usual. He also directed the men in the field not to harm her, because a young foreign woman without any male relatives to protect her risked a very real chance of sexual violence. Boaz ignored social conventions to help and protect an immigrant woman from a hated ethnicity. He recognized her love and devotion for her mother-in-law and honored it. Boaz didn't treat Ruth like a Moabite, but like a neighbor. Ruth and Boaz

eventually married and had a son who was the father of King David, making Ruth the Moabite an ancestor of Jesus Christ.

Immigration is a hot-button issue all over the world. There are more refugees from war, poverty, and violence now than ever before, and the question of who can enter a country's borders and how many can come is highly controversial. Certainly, there are complex issues that need to be addressed in any political decision. However, as followers of the Lord, how we are to treat foreigners and immigrants who are in our midst is clear. Deuteronomy 27:19 says "Cursed is anyone who obstructs the legal rights of immigrants, orphans, or widows." Leviticus 19:34 says "Any immigrant who lives with you must be treated as if they were one of your citizens. You must love them as yourself, because you were immigrants in the land of Egypt; I am the LORD your God." And Jesus himself praised those who cared for strangers, saying "I was hungry and you gave me food to eat. I was thirsty and you gave me a drink. I was a stranger and you welcomed me" (Matthew 25:35).

It's natural to want to protect our own way of life, and sometimes people who are different can disrupt that. Yet, throughout the Bible, it's clear that the value of a human being—any human being—is greater than our own comfort. Jesus often made people uncomfortable by reminding them of that. Perhaps one of the most uncomfortable passages in the New Testament is one often called "The Rich Young Ruler." This story tells of a man who had tried to be righteous his entire life. He asked Jesus what he could do to enter the kingdom of heaven. Jesus told him, "If you want to be complete, go, sell what you own, and give the money to the poor. Then you will have treasure in heaven. And come follow me" (Matthew 19:21). The man sadly left Jesus. He wanted to follow him, but the price was too high.

The simple truth is that as long as there is need in the world, human beings are not keeping the commandments of God. The Gospel of the Nazaraeans, an ancient writing used in the Syrian area by Jewish Christians, had a powerful addition to this story. When the young man told Jesus that he had fulfilled the law, Jesus replied, "How can you say, I have fulfilled the law and the prophets, when it is written in the law; You shall love your neighbor as yourself; and look, many of your neighbors, children of Abraham and Sarah, are covered with filth, dying of hunger, and your house is full of good things, none of which is given to them?"[1]

Where does that put us? Our houses are filled with good things too. A young father once asked me how he could follow Jesus and also be responsible for his family after reading this story. "Would Jesus love me more if I lived in a cardboard box? Is the kingdom of heaven only for the poor?" How can we answer the responsibilities of our faith when Jesus' call is so radical?

The simple answer is that we can't. Jesus tells his disciples in Matthew 19:26 that "It's impossible for human beings. But all things are possible with God." In other words, we are completely dependent on God for our salvation. We fall short, and we only have hope because of the mercy of our Lord. But that doesn't give us an excuse not to try. And if we profess our love of God, then we are invited to devote ourselves to loving our neighbors the best we can as flawed human beings.

That's what Jesus was asking of the rich young ruler—to join in with him. And that's what Jesus asks us to do too. Jesus invites us to see one another as he sees us. We're all human beings who make mistakes, but we are all created by the Lord and are brothers and sisters together trying to navigate a life on this planet. The lines between stranger and native, between rich and poor, and between needing help and being able to give help are always in flux, always changing. There are times we could be on either side of the line, hoping for someone who recognizes us as their neighbor. God asks us to become vulnerable to one another and open to the call of the Lord, living with an open hand when we consider the gifts that God has given us. Discipleship is not something that can be done on the sidelines. It's more than giving money. It's giving one's life to Christ.

How can we imagine the rich young ruler in today's society? Maybe he's a successful businessman, standing before Jesus with an open checkbook, asking, "Okay . . . how much does God want me to give?" Jesus, the champion of the marginalized, stands among his ragged followers and answers, "I want you to become one of us."

1 *The Gospel of Mark in Dialogue* by Ed G. Wallen (Bloomington, Indiana: WestBow Press, 2015).
2 "45 Quotes From Mr. Rogers That We All Need Today" by Geoffrey James (*Inc.com*, Aug. 5, 2019). *https://www.inc.com/geoffrey-james/45-quotes-from-mr-rogers-that-we-all-need-today.html* Accessed Aug. 19, 2020.

Maturing in Faith

Fred Rogers, of *Mister Rogers' Neighborhood*, the children's TV show, dedicated his life to teaching children how to be good neighbors. A Presbyterian preacher, Mr. Rogers taught that every person has something they can contribute to make the world a better place. He wrote, "As human beings, our job in life is to help people realize how rare and valuable each one of us really is, that each of us has something that no one else has—or ever will have—something inside that is unique to all time. It's our job to encourage each other to discover that uniqueness and to provide ways of developing its expression."[2]

Sometimes we encourage another by helping them with basic needs. Sometimes it's listening when they are in pain. Sometimes it's encouraging someone to reach their full potential and strive toward the person God created them to be. There are many ways to build up a person. All of them are ways of loving your neighbor.

Loving your neighbor means respecting the value of others. Truly loving your neighbor means forging relationships in which you all can find joy in each other's uniqueness. It means making unlikely friends, being open to new experiences, and most likely moving a bit out of your comfort zone. True love for another doesn't depend on their "success" to make you feel good.

Fred Rogers also said, "Listening is where love begins: listening to ourselves and then to our neighbors."[2] I would suspect he was talking about listening to the voice of God, the voice of the purest love that speaks to all of us, and then listening to others to see how we can express that love in the world. That would be loving our neighbor in a way truly pleasing to our Lord.

Monday | Psalm 94:1-10

Life can be difficult, and it can seem at times as though God does not see or hear what is happening to us. But this is God's world! God who made our eyes and our ears sees and hears us and will come to our aid and defense. *Lord, I know your justice reigns!*

Tuesday | Isaiah 1:10-18

Those who worship God must be dedicated to justice and helping those in need. Verse 15 says that if hands clasped in prayer are bloody from the neglect of others, God will not listen! Those who turn their backs on the needy are as unclean as if they had defiled themselves. God asks that those who worship make it a priority to do good. *Lord, open my eyes to ways I can serve your people.*

Wednesday | Acts 2:36-42

Peter told his listeners to repent and re-orient themselves to God's vision of the world, not the vision of humans. It was a step into a different way of life. They devoted themselves to the community they built together by learning God's ways, prayer, and fellowship. *Lord, keep me on the pathway of repentance and build my faith within my spiritual community.*

Thursday | Acts 9:26-31

Despite threats on his life, Paul spoke boldly about Jesus Christ. He left a life where he was strong and powerful to suffer for the sake of the gospel. He sacrificed his comfort and security because of the Word, and so that the story of salvation could spread to others. *Lord, may I value your work more than my comfort.*

Friday | Luke 10:1-12

Jesus commissioned workers to spread the good news. This difficult work still remains to be done today, and Jesus said the harvest is plentiful, and the workers are few. Jesus calls us all to be in prayer, to witness, and to bless those who will listen to the gospel story, but to expect failure and danger along the way. *Lord, give me courage to spread your story and perseverance to continue when people reject your word.*

Saturday | James 1:21-27

One cannot only just "talk the talk," but must also "walk the walk." This means living out the commands of Jesus Christ, not speaking evil and caring for those in need. Faith that is only words is worthless and is a deception to both others and to you. *Lord, may my actions reflect my devotion to you.*

Sunday | Acts 6:1-7

God's demands can be broad and far-ranging, and so the community of the Church, with all its varied skills, is needed to fulfill all that God asks of God's believers. Integrity, wisdom, and knowledge of the Spirit are important characteristics of those God calls to serve. *Lord, open my eyes to the work you would have me do for you.*

{ **Key Verse:** Brothers and sisters, carefully choose seven well-respected men from among you. They must be well-respected and endowed by the Spirit with exceptional wisdom. We will put them in charge of this concern. (Acts 6:3) }

SEVEN SELECTED TO SERVE

Lesson: Acts 6:1-7 • **Background:** Acts 2:36-42; 6:1-7; 9:26-31

There is a women's state prison only a few miles from the tiny country church I attend. When the women are released from prison, they are only given twenty dollars and a bus ticket. It can be a nearly impossible situation. Many don't even have a warm coat in the winter. When Kay, a member of our congregation heard about this, she felt God's call to serve these women the best she could. But it was an overwhelming task for one older woman, and so she talked to the church, and the church responded. Now our tiny church runs a busy program called New Journey to give every woman who requests it a wardrobe, toiletries, and basic goods they will need to start a new life upon release. It's not everything they need, but it's more than they had, and the program has expanded in a way that could only be God-driven. It is clearly an example of God using faithful people to do God's work in the world.[1]

From its inception, the Church has been a place where the gospel has been lived out within community. Pentecost is often called the birthday of the Church, when three thousand people responded to Peter's call to repent and be baptized. The Church, until that day, had numbered about 120 people. Peter promised the new believers the gift of the Holy Spirit, and immediately they "devoted themselves to the apostles' teaching, to the community, to their shared meals, and to their prayers" (Acts 2:42). A new community of faith was formed that day, a community held together not by a common ethnic background, economic status, or social standing, but by the love of Jesus Christ and faith in his word.

Faith has the ability to cut across all differences. One of the most remarkable examples was that of Paul. Paul was nothing if not passionate in his beliefs. At one time, he devoted himself to persecuting Christians, believing he was defending his Jewish faith. He even held the coats of the men who stoned Stephen, the first Christian martyr. However, after Jesus spoke to him in a vision, he converted to Christianity. Understandably, Christian believers were frightened of him because of his past, but Barnabas vouched for him and he was accepted into the community of believers. To change one's life as drastically as Paul did is deeply challenging. Christian discipleship in the very best of times is a difficult and demanding path to follow. Paul was supported in his new faith by other Christian believers who validated his experience and encouraged his transformation. Can you imagine what would have happened to Paul and his newfound relationship with Christ if he hadn't had the church to support him? The world would have lost his powerful evangelism, not only through his travels which planted churches all over the known world but through his words we read and study today.

As organizations grow larger, they become more difficult to manage. The Church was no exception. Before Pentecost, it was small enough that everyone knew everyone else's strengths and needs. But as it grew, some people were being neglected. The Church was made up of people from all different backgrounds and walks of life, and one group, the Hellenists, or Greek-speaking believers, felt their needy were being overlooked, not as a result of indifference but because of a poor infrastructure. The Church threatened to divide along lines of ethnicity and language. The informal system of sharing among themselves wasn't enough anymore. They needed to create a way to make sure everyone was served.

So, they created the very first church committee! One gets the feeling that at first, some felt they couldn't be bothered with something as prosaic as food distribution. Teaching the gospel was so much more important! But ignoring other members' needs is not the Christian way. Evangelism is important, but if the people of the church are struggling and suffering, they cannot do the work of the Lord effectively. And so they formed a committee to oversee the daily distribution of food. We know the church leaders were sensitive to the complaints of the Hellenists, as the names of the men chosen to serve on the committee were all Greek. They also gave careful consideration to the committee members' characters. The first church committee was not manned because of experience in food distribution but because of their members' integrity and mature faith. They were chosen because they were "well-respected and endowed by the Spirit with exceptional wisdom" (6:3). Those in the church knew that leaders needed to have a good reputation in order for others to follow them. They also needed to have a connection with the Holy Spirit in order to be guided by God's grace. Exceptional wisdom helps in organizational matters, but it also indicated that their final authority was with the Lord.

So, why be involved with a church today? I've often heard people say their faith is a personal matter, and they don't need to belong to a church to have an effective relationship with God. But these three passages illustrate some of the key reasons God desires believers to be in a faith community.

First, it brings people together. God means the church to be a place where differences don't divide but unify and diversify, and where faith is the strongest connection. It's sad to say that Sunday mornings are still one of the most segregated times in our society, but faith has the ability to overcome this separation. We are all brothers and sisters in Christ, and by living in the Word and devoting ourselves to Christlike living, it is possible to build a community of believers who respond to one another in grace and love, no matter what our backgrounds.

Secondly, a community of believers strengthens, supports, and validates each other's faith. Through corporate study, prayer, and worship, the Church helps each person follow a path of faith that is true to God's Word, supported by the experience of others, strengthened by reason, and upheld by tradition. The Church is an incubator for faith, enabling believers to flourish. Without the support and validation of other believers, it would be very difficult for an individual's faith to survive. And like Paul, this incubator of faith can raise up people who can change the world.

The Church also enables believers to join together in mission. No one in my little country church could run the New Journey program by themselves, but together we have a vibrant and powerful program to help those newly released from incarceration. There are countless other examples of church communities rising up together to not only take care of themselves, but to reach out the larger community and to the world.

In his letter to the Thessalonians, Paul wrote that their church had "work that comes from faith, your effort that comes from love, and your perseverance that comes from hope in our Lord Jesus Christ" (1 Thessalonians 1:3). The Church's vibrant relationship with the Lord is reflected in the faith and work of the members of the church community and is crucial in the life of those God has called out to serve God and to serve the world. God has given God's believers the community of the faithful as a gift to strengthen us, to guide us, and to empower our impact as we serve others. This holy community, set aside to be in service of the Lord, is truly the home of all believers.

1 "New Journey Mission Helps with a Fresh Start" by Page H. Gifford (*Fluvanna Review,* July 26, 2020). *http://fluvannareview. com/2019/04/new-journey-mission-helps-with-a-fresh-start/* Accessed Aug. 19, 2020.

Maturing in Faith

I'll admit it. There have been times in my life when I haven't wanted to go to church. Maybe the preaching didn't speak to me. Maybe I was busy with other things. Maybe I didn't feel as though I was an important part of that spiritual community. And so I took a break from attending.

In March of 2020, many churches took a break from in-person worship in response to the COVID-19 pandemic. Over the next few months, churches began exploring more and more ways to gather online, to maintain their ministries, and to continue their work, even as the pandemic dragged on much longer than any of us expected. As of the writing of this lesson, many churches still find themselves faced with a very difficult question of whether to gather in person or not, as they have discovered that no digital or online experience fully re-creates the experience of in-person worship. For those seeking to feel the presence of the Holy Spirit in a worship service with their community of faith, the seemingly endless task to quarantine grows more and more difficult each day.

We trust the church is created and bound together by the love of the Perfect One, our Lord Jesus Christ. Hebrews 10:24 encourages us by saying, "And let us consider each other carefully for the purpose of sparking love and good deeds." Church is where Christians can support one another, whether we are physically together or not. How lucky are we that we have tools and technology that enable us to communicate and connect with others safely, even when we can't gather in person! Right now, we certainly have to be creative, and nothing we create will be just like it was. Even still, within our community of faith, we can mentor and be mentored, and we can learn to better live out the life we are called to in Jesus Christ.

Monday | Acts 5:27-32, 40-42

God's call is the highest call. Peter's assertion that they must obey God rather than human authority was not a call to anarchy but a protest against the priests' attempts to muzzle the gospel. Empowered by the Holy Spirit, they sought to bring others to salvation. *Lord, may I always answer the highest call from you.*

Tuesday | Luke 7:36-50

Simon didn't think he needed to be forgiven, so he never understood the wonder of grace. Thus, he didn't offer hospitality to Jesus when he came to him. The woman who experienced God's grace and forgiveness worshipped with a grateful heart. Understanding grace and that Jesus has offered it to us is the basis of loving God. *Lord, keep me ever mindful of your gift of grace.*

Wednesday | Romans 2:1-8

Looking inward when attempting to live a godly life is much more important than looking outward. It is crucial to allow the Spirit to expose your own faults to yourself before condemning others for their faults. Live with grace to others as God offers grace to you. *Lord, open my eyes to the parts of me that are disobedient to you.*

Thursday | 2 Thessalonians 3:10-15

Since many early Christians believed Jesus would return very soon, they stopped being responsible. However, God's work is never done. As long as there are people in need, we need to respond as Christians. Our task is always to do what is right. *Lord, encourage me to continue doing your work.*

Friday | 2 Corinthians 1:16-22

God is always and forever faithful. This is the great "Yes" of our relationship. God has proven God's love and care for us through Jesus Christ, who has said "Yes" to our forgiveness, our inclusion in the family of God, and our salvation. *Praise to you, O Lord, for your never-ending faithfulness and hesed, your everlasting love!*

Saturday | Matthew 13:53-58

Familiarity can breed contempt, just like it did for Jesus in Nazareth. But Jesus is woven into the fabric of everyday life, just as he was there. Sometimes the work of Jesus seems too familiar to be divine, but recognizing the ordinary miracles in everyday life opens our eyes to how Christ is around us always. *Lord, open my eyes to the marvels you create every day.*

Sunday | Mark 2:1-12

These friends must have loved their paralytic friend to have gone to such lengths to bring him to Jesus, and Jesus honored them for it. Because of them, their friend was not only healed physically but spiritually. They saw the need of their friend, believed that Jesus could heal him, and did everything they could to bring them together. *Lord, open my eyes to ways I can help a friend who is in need of you.*

Key Verses: Some people arrived, and four of them were bringing to him a man who was paralyzed. They couldn't carry him through the crowd, so they tore off part of the roof above where Jesus was. When they had made an opening, they lowered the mat on which the paralyzed man was lying. (Mark 2:3-4)

TRUE NEIGHBORS

Lesson: Mark 2:1-12 • **Background:** Mark 2:1-12; Matthew 9:1-8; Luke 5:17-26

My son has mastered the art of being a good friend. When his close friend, devastated by the end of his marriage, moved into a dingy little apartment, my son painted it and bought some cheery furnishings at a thrift shop while his friend was at work. When his friend came home, he was gratified by the difference in his new surroundings. He knew he had support to help him through a difficult time.

The familiar Gospel story in these passages tells the story of four good friends of a paralyzed man. Like my son, they were doing their best to help him, but I think watching their attempt must have been quite humorous. Upon Jesus' return to Capernaum, he was again beset by crowds of people. As he taught inside a home, four men attempted to bring their paralyzed friend to him for healing. The crowds were so thick, they could not get near to him. Undaunted, they thought of a creative solution! The homes in that region often had ladders to flat roofs, which were used as an additional work or living area. Surrounded by a sea of people, these four men navigated the crowds, then hoisted a pallet with the paralyzed man up a ladder to the roof. Digging through the mud and thatch roof, they made a hole large enough for their friend to be lowered down. By this time, those underneath them certainly figured out what they were doing—the noise and then the falling roof materials must have created quite a mess and been an interruption to Jesus' teaching. This was a quite a production. Imagine the reaction of the homeowner! It was most likely a terrifying experience for the paralytic too. But these friends were determined. They had heard the stories that this Jesus could heal, and they wanted it for their friend.

But even after all this, there was still some controversy ahead. Ancient Israel had its share of "wonder-workers" who went around claiming to heal people, but they weren't the Son of God. The friends may have thought Jesus was a "wonder-worker" because their faith was in Jesus' ability to heal. But when Jesus saw their faith—not only that of the paralytic but of his friends too—he didn't heal just his legs but healed his soul, saying, "Child, your sins are forgiven!" (2:5). Immediately, the scribes (those that study religious law) got upset. This was

a serious violation of their understanding. Sin is an offense against God. Therefore, only God can pardon sin. How could this Jesus lavish forgiveness on this man? That was like Jesus saying he was God! This was blasphemy—the same charge that was leveled against Jesus at his later trial. They mistook Jesus' care of this man's soul as a slight against God.

Jesus then asked the scribes, "Which is easier—to say 'Your sins are forgiven,' or 'Get up, take your bed, and walk'?" Of course, it's easier to say that a person's sins are forgiven, even if it's something only God can do. That's an internal change and isn't subject to visual verification. Physicians can heal the body, but since they seemed to believe that healing of the body would be proof of healing of the soul, Jesus announced he would heal the body as well. If he was able to heal the man of his physical ailments, then the scribes would have to recognize his authority over sin. And so Jesus did, and the man stood and walked out the door. The man was wholly healed—not only his body, but his spiritual being as well. Jesus was the physician of the body and of the soul.

This is the kind of healing offered by Jesus. While few of us are paralyzed physically, we all have some aspect of our lives where we are crippled at least a little bit. There's something in our life that keeps us from living to our very greatest potential, with purpose and dignity and in complete fellowship with one another. We often think of sin as an action or a character flaw, but sin is bigger than any one person's deeds. Sin is anything active in the world that opposes the will of God, and as no one has a perfect life before God, we all are prey to the terrible things sin can do in our lives. When Jesus forgave the paralytic's sins, he was taking on a foe that takes much more than the life of a limb; he was taking on a foe that attacks the spirit of life itself and the core of our relationship with our Creator.

It's significant that Jesus sent the man home. That is the pattern of healings all throughout the Gospels. One of the most significant examples is Mark 5:18-20, where Jesus cures a demon-possessed man by sending the evil spirits into a herd of pigs. The man pleaded with Jesus to take him with him so that he could be his disciple, but Jesus sent him home. "Go home to your own people," he told him, "and tell them what the Lord has done for you and how he has shown you mercy." The man became an evangelist for Jesus, spreading the good news and bringing many in his region to Christ. This is a reminder that when Christ has healed something in our lives—be it physical, emotional, spiritual, or relational—Jesus wants us to go back into our homes and our normal existence and demonstrate to others what Jesus has done for us.

Within this passage is the first time that Jesus refers to himself as the Human One, often translated as the Son of Man. Much has been written on this phrase and what Jesus meant by it, and nothing is definitive. Jesus typically referred to himself by this phrase in the Book of Mark, although no one else ever did. In some places in the Old Testament, the phrase "the Human One" or "Son of Man" simply means *human being*. A good example of this is Psalm 8:4 which reads in the Revised Standard Version:

"What is man that thou art mindful of him,
And the son of man that thou dost care for him?"

The word in question in Hebrew is 'enosh, which literally translates as "son of man." In the Old Testament, Ezekiel was addressed as 'enosh more than eighty times. However, in the Book of Daniel, 'enosh gains added significance. In Daniel 7:13-14, Daniel had a vision where he saw 'enosh coming with the clouds of heaven and is given everlasting dominion and glory and kingship so that all peoples should serve him. Thus, 'enosh here is an everlasting king over all people who rescues the righteous from persecution. It has been suggested that Jesus chose this title for himself because of the ambiguity of the word, in keeping with his secretive nature about his identity. Those who knew who he was would understand the reference in Daniel, while others would see him simply as a human being. In this way, 'enosh could be understood to reflect both the human and divine natures of Christ.

The friends of the paralytic didn't let anything stand in their way in bringing their friend to Jesus Christ. Their faith was demonstrated in their certainty that Jesus would heal their friend and by their perseverance in getting through to Jesus. But their friend got much more than he bargained for. By forgiving his sins, Jesus removed the barriers that had grown between the man and a true relationship with God. His friends didn't just help him find strengthened legs, but a new life through a relationship with the Son of God who was living on earth as the Human One.

Maturing in Faith

What do you think the former paralytic said to his friends as they walked home together? First, I think he'd be overwhelmed with gratitude. His friends had persevered for him. They didn't turn away when they saw the crowds, but found a creative solution to bring him to Christ. It was a bold thing to do. They risked being ridiculed. What would a teacher think about his lesson being interrupted by someone lowered down in front of him? They dared to interrupt Jesus for their friend. But they had faith. They believed Jesus could heal him.

And here was their friend, walking—yes, walking!—beside them, going home. Not only that, he had a new perspective on his entire life, having been forgiven and blessed by Christ himself. It was worth all the risk because their friend had been healed, both body and soul.

While Jesus doesn't always heal the easy thing, the body, he has told us that all we have to do to be healed spiritually is ask. But it still takes work on our part to be whole spiritually. It takes perseverance to stay on the path of faithfulness once Christ has shown you the way. It takes boldness to change one's life for Christ. It takes courage to ask Jesus into your life. But most of all, it takes faith that Jesus really can heal the pain in one's life. But like the paralytic in this story, one of the greatest gifts we can be given are other believers in Christ to help carry us when we feel weak. It is through the support of other believers that God works to strengthen faith. May each one of us be a support for other believers in need.

PRAYER

"If one more person suggests to me that I should pray the Psalms, I may punch them in the face." That was probably as good a proof as any that I really needed to be praying the Psalms. I was in one of those dark nights of the soul (see a lesson in this series) when I felt deeply disconnected from God. I could not form the words. Actually, if I am honest, I didn't want to talk to God. Really, what could God say to me anyway that would make me feel better? No, I needed things fixed, and God wasn't going to do that, so what was there to talk about?

Sometimes we don't have the words. Sometimes we have too many words. And sometimes those words are not clean and pretty. They are backed by rage. They are backed by hurt. They are backed by utter and complete sadness. They don't feel like words we should bring to God, which is exactly why we should bring them to God. I am fond of telling people, "Go ahead. Yell at God. God's got big pants on. God can take it." Getting up the nerve to do that, however . . . sometimes that takes a bit.

We see that happen in Job. Job starts out calmly sitting through his loss, praising God and affirming God's goodness. As the loss grows, however, Job gets less and less nice. He starts to moan and bewail his own state, and then to criticize and taunt God. The gloves are coming off as this book goes further along. And Job is naming that reality right to the ear of God.

There is something to be said for praying the Psalms, and particularly the psalms of lament. They give us the words we sometimes can't muster. But they also let us join the chorus of humanity. We all suffer. We all ache. And we all need to name that reality to God. And when we do it together, we feel that much less alone.

—Michelle J. Morris

Monday | Psalm 3:1-8
In this psalm, the psalmist was totally surrounded! There was nothing he could do to save himself—nothing, that is, except to pray. But he trusted in the protection of the Lord who sustained him. Even though thousands sought to attack him, he was not afraid. *Lord, deliver me from danger and teach me not to fear.*

Tuesday | Numbers 22:20-35
Balaam was hired by the Midians to curse the Hebrew people, but God forbid him to go. When he went in defiance of God's commands, he became adversarial to God. This passage uses the word *satan* in Hebrew to describe Balaam because he disobeyed. Only his donkey saved him! *Lord, may I be obedient to your will and never become your adversary.*

Wednesday | 1 Chronicles 21:1-8
Satan tempted David and uncovered his weakness. By taking a census to find out the number of his fighting men, David showed a lack of trust in the Lord. David depended on his own knowledge and ability to make his decisions instead of following the guidance of God. To David's credit, he realized his sin and asked for forgiveness. *Lord, help me to withstand the temptation to sin.*

Thursday | Zechariah 3:1-10
In Zechariah's vision, Joshua symbolized the sinful Israel standing before the Lord. Satan, the adversary, hurled accusation after accusation at him, but the Lord offered him mercy. Dressing him in clothes of righteousness, God forgave Israel's sins. The Lord's mercy overcame the accusations of Satan. *Oh, Lord, I praise you for your great mercy when I only deserve condemnation.*

Friday | Job 1:1-5
Job was described as perfectly righteous. This passage said he had not sinned at all. Every aspect of his life was blessed and complete. Later, when Job's friends challenged him and said he must have done something to deserve God's punishment, Job could honestly say he was innocent and could not be blamed for his suffering. *Lord, help me to live an innocent life, like Job.*

Saturday | Job 1:6-12
Why do we obey God? Is it because we love God or is it because of what God can do for us? Satan believed that Job loved the blessings God gave him more than he loved God, and challenged God to test Job's loyalty. *Lord, may my dedication to you be for who you are, not what you can do for me.*

Sunday | Job 1:13-20
After Job learned of his devastating losses, he sat in the ashes and praised God. His love for God didn't depend on his position in life. He loved God for who God is, regardless of Job's situation. Job passed the test and was able to praise God, even in the midst of great personal grief. *Lord, may I give you glory in any situation.*

Key Verse: Job arose, tore his clothes, shaved his head, fell to the ground, and worshipped. (Job 1:20)

JOB'S RESPONSE TO SUFFERING: WORSHIP

Lesson: Job 1:8-20 • Background: Job 1:1-20; Psalm 3:1-8

"Those who pursue righteousness and kindness will find life, righteousness, and honor" (Proverbs 21:21). Those are good words to live by. Loving God and loving neighbor is what God asks of us, and throughout the Scriptures, there are stories of people who are rewarded for following this advice. That's because this advice is generally true. In most cases, obeying God and pursuing righteousness will result in a happy life that is rich and blessed.

Except when it's not true. Tragedies affect godly people just as much as wicked ones. Good people get sick, have terrible accidents, or are affected by natural disasters. They can be ruined financially or lose a beloved family member. Righteousness is not a protection against the heartbreaks of this world. But why not? Why do bad things happen to good people?

This is the central question in the Book of Job, and it is a question people have asked since the very beginning of our faith. Job is thought to be the oldest book in the entire Bible. It's written in a folktale manner, even beginning with the biblical equivalent of "Once upon a time." It's the "Yes, but!" to the sentiments in the Wisdom books, written before that wisdom was ever formally recorded. It examines how God interacts in the world and explores the relationship that human beings have with our Creator. Job is a brilliant theological discourse which is challenging and insightful for all believers.

The beginning of the Book of Job is pretty difficult to accept. The reader is introduced to the absolute perfect man, Job. He is blameless, pious, and upright. He is blessed with wealth and children. He is wealthy in all three areas of commerce at the time: his oxen and donkeys are used for agriculture, his wealth in graze land is reflected in the amount of sheep he owns, and his camels are used for trade. Even the numbers of his family and possessions symbolize wholeness and perfection. He is so righteous that he sacrifices just in case his children inadvertently offend God.

His perfection catches the attention of The Satan. It's important to realize that the character of The Satan is quite different than the evil devil we ascribe to the name Satan now. The Satan (with the article "The") was an office or position in the heavenly council and meant "the accuser or adversary." His job was to find people who were disloyal to God and then to defend God's honor by bringing their misdeeds to God's attention. It is only in later writings that the character of The Satan became "Satan," who was opposed to God. The Book of Zechariah also mentions The Satan, and it is thought that this literary character may have been modeled from spies of the king in the Persian court.

The Satan questions Job's motives for being so righteous, saying that if God withdrew Job's blessings, Job would then curse God. The Satan says that it is only because of the good things God has given Job that Job praises God. He asks to try to uncover Job's true character and see what would happen if Job lost everything. God agrees to the challenge, with just one stipulation. The Satan can take everything that Job has, except his health.

The Satan does a good job of withdrawing God's blessings. Alternating between enemy attacks and natural disasters, The Satan destroys Job's oxen and donkeys, his sheep, his camels, and finally, his family. In each case, only one servant is spared the decimation in order to bring the terrible news to Job. They arrive one right after the other, not even allowing the first to finish his story before another servant shows up with the next disaster story. There are four disasters, the number four being a symbol of completeness, which completely destroys everything Job had.

Why does God allow that to happen to Job? This question is one of the most difficult issues many people have with the Book of Job. However, it helps to remember that this story is in essence a folktale. The Bible doesn't hide this story's fictional nature. It's constructed as an examination of righteous suffering. As such, the beginning of the book is a setup for the lessons to come, lessons that challenge the concept of a barter religion. Most ancient religions and much faith today work on a barter system with God. People pray the right prayers, give the right sacrifices, and perform the right rituals in order to have God on their side. Good people get blessings. Bad people get punished. God behaves in a prescribed way, protecting from harm those who worship and obey correctly. This kind of theology implies that followers have a contract with God, and they try to guarantee their comfort, security, and position by adhering to religious formulas. This belief is still popular today. It only takes a quick search online to find many books that instruct people how to pray properly to activate blessings, what to do to quickly change your life through blessings from God, and even how to pray so that God will make you financially secure. However, this kind of faith falls apart when a person believes they've been following the rules, and bad things still happen. It's why the beginning of the Book of Job is so disturbing. God doesn't follow the contract. Imagine what the challenge of The Satan would have done to Job if this was what he believed!

In the first chapter of Job, God wins the first round. Job is devastated and goes into deep mourning, tearing his clothing and shaving his head, both symbols of deep sorrow. But unlike the predictions of The Satan, he doesn't curse God. In fact, he worships God. Stoically, he says that as he came into the world with nothing, everything that he once had was a gift from God, and it is completely up to God to take it away. Despite his deep grief, he continues to praise God and trusts that God will protect him and help him. Psalm 3 is probably a good insight to his thoughts at that time. Attributed to King David as he was fleeing from his murderous son Absalom, the psalm acknowledges human vulnerability but confidently calls for God's help. Job would not abandon the Lord that quickly. He is able to worship God, even in the most painful of situations.

During World War II, many Polish priests were sent to German concentration camps for speaking against the Third Reich. Despite the horrific conditions and strict regulations against any type of religious worship, many of those priests held secret worship services. Their faith was not dependent on their own comfort or safety, but was based on the knowledge of the Lord God. There were no conditions on their love for God. In a faith that is not barter-driven, God doesn't bestow blessings because they have been earned or they are owed, but because they are gifts. Removing any thought of being owed anything from God allows one to find God in any situation, good or bad, and allows one to truly understand the blessings of forgiveness, salvation, and grace.

That is what Job is able to do in the first chapter. Job worships God not because of what God could do for him, but because of who God is. God's assessment of Job's character is correct. Job's blessings were not the cause of his faith and devotion to God.

1 "It Is Well with My Soul," by Horatio G. Spafford, 1873 (*The United Methodist Hymnal,* 1989), p. 377.

Maturing in Faith

The famous Chicago fire tore through the city in 1871, financially ruining many people, including a wealthy lawyer named Horatio Spafford. Soon after that, his four-year-old son died of pneumonia. Then, in 1873, his wife and four daughters boarded the SS Ville du Havre sailing for Europe. He was to join them a few weeks later. During the crossing, the ship collided with another ship. His wife sent back the heartbreaking telegram, "Saved alone, what shall I do?" All four of his young daughters had drowned.

As he made the ocean crossing to join his wife, the captain of his ship called him out to the bow as they crossed the place where his daughters had perished. Looking into the dark waters, he wrote the words to the immortal hymn, "It Is Well with My Soul":

> whatever my lot, thou hast taught me to say,
> It is well, it is well with my soul.[1]

Praising God in the midst of sorrow doesn't mean the sorrow is any less. Like Job, Spafford's grief was crushing. But praising God means that we know that God is with us in all things. God walks with us through the valley of the shadow of death, through the fear of illness, and through the loss of financial security. Praising God in the midst of sorrow means taking comfort in the presence of the Lord, knowing God's loving arms are around us.

When the coronavirus raged in Italy, people stood on their balconies, singing and making music together, despite being quarantined in their homes. They were celebrating life, unity with their neighbors, and hope for an end to the pandemic. This is the praise we can find in the midst of sorrow, in the depths of despair when we look to God for hope and deliverance.

Monday | Psalm 139:19-24

This psalmist is a realist and knows there will always be those who work against God and God's people. The world would be so much better without them! But nothing is black and white. The psalmist needs to be examined by God and led on the right path. *Lord, search me and keep me from falling into sin.*

Tuesday | 1 Samuel 3:10-21

Eli's sons corrupted temple worship, and so the Lord announced the end of his family's place in the temple. Eli accepted this harsh judgment because it was necessary to remove the sin brought by his sons. His humble acceptance made way for a new beginning for the people of Israel. *Lord, remove those things that impede your will, even if it be me.*

Wednesday | John 18:1-11

Jesus knew what the Father had in store for him and accepted the suffering he would bear for the salvation of the world. When the soldiers arrived, Jesus stepped forward and identified himself as the one to be arrested by saying "I Am," identifying himself as the Lord of all. *Thank you, Jesus, for your model of following God's will.*

Thursday | Acts 21:1-14

The Spirit told Paul to go to Jerusalem, and he obeyed the call, even though he knew he would suffer for it. Following the will of God was the most important thing he could do, even though he knew he would be arrested, bound, and thrown in prison. *Lord, may my priority always be your will.*

Friday | Job 1:21-22

Everything we have comes from the Lord—all our possessions, our health, the people we love, even life itself. We cannot hold on to any of it ourselves. God is the director of all that happens, and by letting go of what we can't really control anyway, we can bless the Lord in all times and circumstances. *Lord, help me to hold the things you have given me with an open hand and praise you in all things.*

Saturday | Job 2:1-6

What would cause you to turn from God? The Satan took all of Job's children and possessions, but Job still praised God. Then The Satan challenged God further, saying that a person would give up all integrity to save their own life. The Satan could not believe Job would value his relationship with God more than his own survival. *Lord, may you be my first priority always.*

Sunday | Job 2:7-10

The Satan was permitted to afflict Job with a terrible skin disease. Job's wife believed that Job's integrity was worthless because God did not protect him. She asked what the point was in worshipping a God who would allow such horrors? Yet Job remained steadfast—at least in his words. *Lord, protect my integrity and help me to trust you in all things.*

> **Key Verse:** [Job] said: "Naked I came from my mother's womb; naked I will return there. The LORD has given; the LORD has taken; bless the LORD's name." (Job 1:21)

JOB'S RESPONSE TO SUFFERING: RESIGNATION

Lesson: Job 1:21-22; 2:7-10 • Background: Job 1:21-22; 2:1-10; Psalm 139:19-24

Many people just know the prologue of the Book of Job, which are these first two chapters. It's easy to tell if someone has never read the rest of the book if they talk about "the patience of Job." Patience is certainly what we've seen so far in the story. Job is submissive and pious, even with his extreme suffering. These two chapters are a very simplistic view of Job that make his faith and integrity seem impossible to model oneself after. Who wouldn't be angry with God in these circumstances, especially as we know the backstory, the deal with The Satan? Doesn't God deserve some questions? But the first two chapters of the Book of Job don't answer questions. They raise them. The Book of Job was written to examine our relationship with God in the real world, where innocents die, where life isn't fair, and where good people suffer. The answers that will be given will come later.

Job's stoic answer to his initial tragedies is that the Lord gave him all that he had and so, therefore, the Lord could take it all back. In a dualistic view of the world, one usually praises God for what is good and blames evil for what is bad, but Job recognizes the right of God to even destroy that which is good and still deserve praise. His pious response means God has won the initial duel with The Satan, but The Satan returns to God and challenges him again. "Let me attack his body," The Satan says. "Then he will curse you! People will do anything to save their own lives!" God readily agrees, shockingly so, only with the provision that Job will not die. The Satan then afflicts Job with a terrible skin disease that affects him from head to foot. Skin diseases were especially reviled in ancient times and thought to be a sign of God's displeasure, so not only is his pain physical, but he suffers social ostracization as well. As he sits in the ashes from mourning the death of his children, he scrapes the scabs off his skin with a broken piece of pottery. It's hard to visualize a more pathetic, heartbreaking fate for a man who was once called the greatest of all the people of the East.

Even his wife can't bear it. To her, Job's integrity has become worthless. His righteousness does nothing for him. God doesn't protect him, his children, or his possessions. He clearly doesn't deserve his fate, and it seems both hopeless and foolish to continue to honor a God who would allow him to suffer as he does. Job's wife believes God deserves to be cursed, and encourages Job to do so, even if it would mean his death. Certainly, God would destroy anyone who outright cursed God, but in this case, that defiant act of self-destruction would be preferable to continuing as he is. It would be a final act of dignity for Job to curse a God who would allow him to suffer like that after the many years of devotion and praise.

Yet, Job refuses. He has gladly accepted the good times, and now he has to accept his troubles as well. He remains sitting in the ashes of his pain and suffering. The text says he does not sin with his lips, but that begs the question: What is he thinking? Is Job questioning the justice of God in his heart? The theologian Bruce Birch states that these first two chapters of the Book of Job raise four important questions about our relationship with God and our place within creation.

The first question deals with a faith based on reward and retribution, which we discussed last week. The Book of Proverbs and many of the psalms speak of God showering down blessings for righteous living and destroying the wicked. For the most part, these Wisdom Scriptures tell us how life works. Honesty pays. Kindness is repaid with kindness. Cruel people lose in the end. The Torah is God's rulebook for a happy life, and it really is the best way to live. The wisdom that equates right living with blessing is almost always true. Almost. The Book of Job honestly confronts when life is not fair.

Secondly, does God really seek to protect God's people, or is the outcome simply arbitrary? It seems God made this deal with The Satan without regard for Job at all. How do we square a God of love with a God that allows chaos and random events that can devastate innocent people? As I write this, I sit in quarantine, having been exposed to the coronavirus. Why would God allow a worldwide pandemic? What saves one person and not another?

Thirdly, if a man with as much integrity as Job is left to suffer, what is the point of obeying God? Being obedient to God's Word is a demanding way of living.

Why should we attempt to serve God if suffering could be part of the deal for even the most righteous among us?

Lastly, if we believe all things come from God, how do we reconcile evil things? Why would God allow evil in a world created for his beloved children? What do we really mean when we speak of the justice of God in light of these questions?

Although the character of Job seems simplistic and overly accepting of his fate in these first two chapters, he emerges as a very complex being who struggles with these questions too. The famous patience of Job really only lasts the first two chapters! That's a really good thing, actually, because it removes the shadow of guilt believers might have for not dealing with adversity with the stoic acceptance and piety that is usually attributed to Job. Conversely, God also emerges as a much more complex being. They both come to terms with what it means to be the Creator and the created, and what it truly means to be in covenant with one another.

While the idea of Job's patience may not be accurate, his commitment to his relationship with God truly was the central part of his life. He never questioned the existence of God, the power of God, and the ability God had to impact his life. His faith was strong enough that he never considered abandoning his connection with God; rather, the important thing for him was to understand, as much as he was able, the relationship between himself and the Creator of the universe.

No wonder the Book of Job is known for being so difficult. It challenges us with some of the most demanding questions of our faith, our commitment to God, and our place within God's creation. It is not a complete vision of our relationship with God, as it doesn't speak of God's great love for us or God's deep interactions with each one of us as individuals. But it does face, head-on, the challenging questions about the suffering of the righteous and how each of us can continue to find peace and comfort in a relationship with our Creator God.

At the end of the prologue, Job sits, resigned and defeated, in the ashes of his despair. He is willing to accept everything God could do to him, whether it was blessing him or cursing him. He might be too numb at that moment to ask the questions that would plague him for the rest of the story. Those questions would come later, after his "friends," who worshipped God not for who God is but for what God could do for them, accused Job of evildoing as the cause of his suffering.

Maturing in Faith

The first two chapters of the Book of Job, simply put, are shocking. They don't give comfort, and they don't assure us of a God who is always there for us. We don't read of God's *hesed*, God's steadfast, ever-enduring love for us. Instead, we read of a devoted, faithful man who is used as a pawn in God's game with The Satan.

But the Book of Job isn't the only place we read about a God who is confusing and disturbing. Almost one-third of the psalms are songs of lament, where the psalmist cries out in pain and suffering, wondering why God has allowed them to be in such difficult and dangerous situations. Read Psalms 13; 22; 30; 88; or 139 for examples. The fact that these questions and emotions are included in our Scriptures mean they are legitimate questions of our faith, and it means God is big enough to take the questions.

Job had lost everything, but stubbornly, he still hung on to his belief in God's justice, mercy, and sovereignty. There is something deeply admirable in Job's determination. His relationship with God, even in the depths of his frustration, anger, and pain, was of such value that he didn't turn away. He knew his relationship with God was still life-sustaining.

It's also important to remember that the Book of Job does not tell the whole story. Despite the suffering in the world, we worship a God who has promised over and over again that we are loved with an everlasting love, and that our salvation was worth the sacrifice of God's beloved Son. There is much to learn by studying these Scriptures, but we should never forget the character of our Lord, and that even though there is suffering, we can be certain of the grace and love of our God.

Monday | Psalm 43:1-5

The psalmist cried out because he was falsely accused, but unlike Job, he called for God to deliver him. Although he hadn't yet been rescued, he anticipated God's help and looked forward to praising God in the temple. His hope for deliverance was in the Lord. *Lord, may I continue to hope in you, even in the midst of injustice and fear.*

Tuesday | Job 2:11-13

Job's friends grieved in silence with him for a week. Often, the presence of others is the greatest comfort because it shows compassion for another's pain without reservation. It was the best thing they did for him, because once they opened their mouths, they attacked him. *Lord, help me to be a true comfort to others in pain, and teach me to swallow hurtful words.*

Wednesday | Job 4:1-9

Eliphaz reminded Job that Job had helped others who were suffering, and now he could expect God to help him. Eliphaz believed a person's integrity was related to his well-being. To Eliphaz, Job's cries of anguish betrayed a lack of trust in the relationship of blessings for good deeds in which Eliphaz believed. *Lord, may I be able to share another's cries of anguish without judgment.*

Thursday | Job 11:13–12:5

Neither Zophar nor Job believed there could be anything chaotic within the world. Therefore, Zophar was sure Job was guilty of sin. For Job, God was cruel and uncaring. When Zophar told Job his life would be wonderful if he didn't sin, Job satirically retorted he had become a laughingstock to those who believed they were wise. *Lord, help me to accept what is chaotic in the world.*

Friday | Job 19:1-6

By insisting Job must have sinned, his friends were humiliating and belittling him. If Job had inadvertently sinned, that was between himself and God, even if Job felt God was in the wrong. Once again, he begged them to stop tormenting him. *Lord, may I be compassionate to those who are suffering.*

Saturday | Job 19:7-19

Everything Job once valued was taken from him. One of the most painful things for him to lose was the regard others once had for him, which left him alone throughout this ordeal. His entire social network failed him, and he blamed God for his rejection and isolation. *Lord, give me the eyes to see the lonely and those who need friendship while going through difficult times.*

Sunday | Job 19:20-27

Job's only hope was that there would be someone, someday, who would take up his case and defend him before God. He wanted his words recorded so that one day he would be vindicated. As followers of Jesus Christ, we know we have a mediator who will take up our sins and allow us to stand before God. *Thanks be to Jesus Christ, our Mediator and Redeemer!*

Key Verses: If you look down on me and use my disgrace to criticize me, know then that God has wronged me and enclosed his net over me.
(Job 19:5-6)

JOB'S RESPONSE TO SUFFERING: PROTEST

Lesson: Job 19:1-6, 13-19 • **Background:** Job 19:1-27; Psalm 43:1-5

At the end of chapter two in the Book of Job, Job is passively sitting amid ashes, telling his wife they should accept the good with the bad. But in today's passage, Job has had more time to digest the tragedies that upset his life. Chapter three in the Book of Job is a heartrending cry by Job for God to pity him. He cries out for his death, even regretting he has ever been born. In the following chapters, his friends arrive to comfort him, but their comfort quickly turns to accusations. Their faith is centered on God giving blessings for righteousness and punishing sinners, so their only explanation for Job's dire situation is that he must have sinned, somewhere. They counsel him to admit his guilt and humbly take God's direction. Bildad defends God's actions in Job 8:3, saying, "Does God pervert justice, or does the Almighty distort what is right?" In chapter 15:4-5, Eliphaz tells Job, "You are truly making religion ineffective and restraining meditation before God. Your mouth multiplies your sins a thousand times." After Job has lost everything, they are bent on taking his integrity too.

That was the easy solution to the problem of suffering for them, as it is for us today. If people always deserve what happens to them, then no one has to worry about disaster befalling them if they are responsible. If someone gets sick, it's because they didn't take care of themselves. If someone has a financial setback, it's because they're careless with money. If someone has difficulties with a relationship, it's because of a personal failing. All someone has to do to be healthy and successful is follow the rules. We are in control. People are uncomfortable around suffering people who assert their innocence. It questions the system of inherent justice, of right and wrong that our society is based upon. It's much easier to just blame the victim.

Sometimes we do cause our own trouble, but certainly not all the time. In Job's case, he didn't cause his problems, but his "friends" didn't accept that. Almost all of chapter 19 is a plea from Job for them to stop humiliating and accusing him of wrongdoing; in effect, kicking him when he was down. Everyone turned against him, from his "friends" to his family. The guests living in his house, usually people grateful for hospitality, ignored him. His servants didn't answer him. Even his wife was repulsed by him. His breath, which can also be translated as his spirit, was offensive to her. But worse than all of that, he believed God had turned against him too. These passages are full of bitterness and anger toward God. God's actions against him seemed completely over the top. Job was once the greatest man in the east, but God had entrapped him, stripping him of his crown, and set forces against him like a general sending vast troops into battle as he sat in his humble tent.

The colorful phrase "escaped by the skin of my teeth" is from Job 19:20, but in context, doesn't tell of escape at all. Instead of being written "by the skin of my teeth," a better translation would be "escaped only with the skin of my teeth." As no one has skin on their teeth, it really means he escaped with nothing. Even with nothing, he still couldn't get pity from his "friends"! They would not risk taking sides with someone whom even God had forsaken.

Job, as many psalmists and the author of Lamentations did, complained in faith to God. They dared to display their pain and anger, but this kind of honest prayer allowed them to fully open their hearts to God. It was because they valued their relationship with God that they "took God on" and demanded answers to their suffering. Job could not have been angry with God if he gave up his belief in God. While his anger and accusation against God might seem shocking, his resistance meant he kept hope that the entire system was not corrupt, and that there was a way to make it right. He didn't sink into passivity and give up the will to fight. He longed to be exonerated and for his name to be honored once again. It didn't even really matter if it happened after his death. He was so certain anyone really listening to him would be convinced of his innocence that verses 23 and 24 speak of his desire for his words to be recorded. His wish moved quickly from someone to write his words of innocence on a scroll to inscribing them on lead and finally to engraving them on a rock. Each successive wish was a more permanent way of recording his struggles. The reason he wanted his words recorded was so someone, sometime, somewhere would read them and then stand up for his innocence. He was hoping for his *go'el* or Redeemer.

Verse 25 is perhaps the most well-known verse in the entire Book of Job. It's difficult for me to read it without the strains of Handel's "Messiah" running through my mind, and so I immediately associate it with the story of Jesus Christ and the promise of a Redeemer for us all. But the word that is translated as *Redeemer* here is the Hebrew word *go'el*, which can also be translated as "avenger." In ancient times, the *go'el*, sometimes known as the kinsman redeemer, was a close relative who took care of others in his family. For example, Boaz in the story of Ruth was Ruth and Naomi's kinsman redeemer. A *go'el* was obligated to fulfill a legal role for a family, such as taking responsibility for a family debt, assuring their family members were treated justly, or to care for widows and orphans within the family. This word signifies a legal responsibility to an individual and is not interchangeable with the word *Savior*. *Savior* usually applies to a larger group of people and is not limited to legal assistance, like the *go'el*. Job was crying out for someone to take his case up with God and plead his innocence. God was the judge, and Job needed a legal witness to argue his case in the courts of heaven.

We don't know who Job had in mind as his *go'el*, if he even knew himself. Perhaps it would be one of the heavenly host or an avenging angel. Whoever it was, Job was clinging to the hope that somewhere, someone would believe him and stand up for him. He didn't know if it would be after he was dead or while he was still alive, but he desperately wanted someone to make his case before what he believed was a terribly unjust God. He wanted someone to help him "take God on."

It can be disconcerting to understand the original meaning of these verses, especially when the most common exposure to them is within the framework of Handel's great composition, "Messiah." While the word *go'el* and the cultural background of Job are not a prediction of Jesus Christ and specific hope for his redemption, as readers today, we can rest assured we do have a mediator in Jesus, and that the events of the New Testament give this passage a new richness and meaning for us today. Because of what we know now, we can claim these verses as a hope for our exoneration when we suffer from being falsely accused, and know our Lord Jesus Christ will stand in the gap between even our sin and our righteousness before God.

Maturing in Faith

A few years back, I was a terrible friend. I had a close friend who suddenly lost her husband in a tragic accident, and I wasn't there for her as I should have been. When I think about why I failed her, I realized it had to do with my own fear. How would I deal if the same thing happened to me? It was too terrible to consider. And so, I stepped back, not wanting to face the possibility of chaos disrupting my happy little world.

Job's friends didn't step back, but maybe even that would have been better than their reaction. They didn't want to believe that chaos could disrupt their world, too, and so they blamed Job for his tragedies. They were sure he was suffering because of his own actions, because that way, they remained safe. Those tragedies couldn't happen to them because they were being responsible and were righteous before God. It must have been Job's fault.

Blaming the victim is distressingly common in our society. People are poor because of personal failings. People get sick because they don't take care of themselves. Natural disasters happen because God is punishing a nation for something. Every time we look at the problems of others—be it personal problems, societal problems, or just natural disasters—and come up with reasons why it's their fault, we run the risk of being like Job's friends. When we place blame, we're protecting our own illusions of security at the expense of those who suffer.

If we make excuses for other people's problems, not only are we creating a faith that can't withstand our own calamities, but we impinge the integrity of those who suffer. This not only further injures and demeans the one experiencing suffering, but it often gives us an "out"—an excuse—for not stepping in and helping, or for not standing up for systemic changes that prevent the creation of victims in the first place.

Monday | Psalm 44:9-26
How should God's people respond when it feels like God has forgotten them? The people in Psalm 44 were confused and bewildered. Still, they turned to God in prayer, having faith in God's *hesed*, or everlasting love for them. *Lord, when I feel as though you are not listening, assure me that you are there.*

Tuesday | Job 7:1-10
When Job considered the human condition, he saw endless work, pain, and death. It seemed pointless and hopeless, especially once he had lost everything and was in such physical agony. He confronted God with the uselessness of his short, insignificant, and pain-filled life. *Thank you, Lord, that you will listen to my complaints without condemnation.*

Wednesday | Job 7:11-15
Job cried out for God to leave him alone and asked why God bothered to pay attention to human beings. Chapter 30 is a parody of many of the praise psalms, reworking their well-known phrases into "anti-psalms." The words of praise in them sounded hollow and blind to Job's pain. *Lord, may I feel your comfort even when words of comfort sound hollow.*

Thursday | Job 30:1-8
Job, a man who was praised for his compassion, harshly criticized the outcasts of society who mocked him in his pain. Job was distressed by how far he had fallen in the eyes of society, but it is shocking to read how even a compassionate man scorned those who lived on the very edges of humanity. *Lord, may I continue to be compassionate to others, even when I am suffering.*

Friday | Job 30:9-15
The outcasts and scorned people saw Job's catastrophes as an assault from God, and so they felt as though they could also assault him. Job feared for his life at the hands of those he had barely given a second thought before. Because they believed Job was rejected by God, they felt they were justified in their actions. *Lord, help me to keep my compassion for those who are suffering.*

Saturday | Job 30:16-23
Job was in physical agony with nowhere to turn. As he waited for death, God seemed to be tormenting him further. Job felt that God rejected him, just as the social outcasts had done. Even worse, Job accused God of lifting him up on the wind, perhaps alluding to his previous status and wealth, only to make his fall that much greater and more painful. *Help me to be sensitive to the loss of dignity often felt by those who are sick or dying.*

Sunday | Job 30:24-31
Job insisted he was compassionate to those in need, and when the tables were turned, no one was compassionate to him, especially God. He had formed expectations that were not met. He waited for God to be good to him, but all that happened was evil. *Lord, help me to give the compassion I would want to receive.*

Key Verse: Now my life is poured out on me; days of misery have seized me. (Job 30:16)

JOB'S RESPONSE TO SUFFERING: ANGRY DESPAIR

Lesson: Job 30:16-23 • **Background:** Job 30:1-31; Psalm 44:9-26

It was August 1990. My husband was a B-52 pilot in the Air Force and we were stationed in Caribou, Maine. We were parents of two preschoolers and far from any family in a very remote area. Suddenly, Kuwait was invaded and, in less than twelve hours, I stood on a tarmac with my children watching my husband pilot a fully ordnanced B-52 toward a war zone. "When will he come home, Mommy?" my daughter asked me. I didn't know. I didn't know if he would come home at all. I was frightened and angry at God, and a few months later, I wrote these words that I rediscovered recently: "Getting really, truly angry at God is the scariest thing you can do. I yelled at God, and then I was terrified by it. I know that I backed away from those feelings and tried to deny that I ever felt them."

These are the same emotions that Job takes on full force, refusing to back away from them and demanding answers. Job is about to put his case before God for judgment in chapter 31. In ancient times, an accused person who was falsely accused would go before a judge and swear his or her innocence. This was taken very seriously. It was assumed that if this oath was a lie, something horrible would happen to the oath-taker, so even the most hardened criminal would hesitate before taking a false oath. The responsibility would then move to the accuser to prove they had not slandered the accused. By taking this oath of clearance, Job is demanding God answer for Job's mistreatment.

Job justifies his reasons for taking such a drastic step. The first fifteen verses are a heartbreaking account of his fall from dignity and respect. In bitter, stinging language, Job describes the most outcast of society who have found him an object of their contempt. In a culture where social position was the most important characteristic about a person, Job has fallen from the very peak of respectability to a place where even those who were driven out of society to live as rejects in the desert would spit in his face. For a man who spoke of his compassion for the poor, his description of these people is shockingly harsh. The point, however, is not that he is unmerciful, but that he is profoundly rejected by all of society, even those who are on the very bottom rungs. He is traumatized by their treatment of him. Job was born into comfort and wealth, and now that he has become an outcast, even the outcasts are hostile to him. He is rejected by the rejects of society in a culture where social position is everything.

Even his own body turns against him. His pain, especially at night, is like rats gnawing at his bones. He is tormented and strangled by his clothing. Verse 19 accuses God of throwing him into the mud or mire, back into the dirt from which God originally crafted human beings back in Genesis. This is a final rejection by God, thrown back as trash into the lifeless mud that once formed him. He has completely lost his identity as a human being.

Because of all he has suffered, Job demands justice. He cries out that he has helped those in trouble, and God hasn't helped him. The insinuation is that he has behaved better than God! God has been cruel to him, Job argues, by repaying his good with evil. Job's pleas are ignored. God has stopped responding. The only thing left for Job to do is to formally make an oath of innocence and call God to trial.

Psalm 44 echoes many of Job's emotions. It's unknown when the psalm was written, but clearly Israel was suffering profound military defeat. Because the psalmist seemed confused and bewildered as to why God had abandoned them, commentators don't believe it was related to the defeat of the Babylonian Exile. Israel knew they had worshipped foreign gods then and suffered their defeat as a well-deserved punishment. But this psalm, like Job, protested innocence. Verse 18 cries out, "Our hearts haven't turned away, neither have our steps strayed from your way." They clearly believed it was God's fault that they were being slaughtered, and the psalmist pleaded for God to wake up. Like Job, they rejected a theology which said suffering and disaster were always connected with sin. They clearly had not sinned, and they were suffering anyway!

Job wants an easy resolution to a difficult question. Job's friends try to give him answers, suggesting he is wrong in believing he is innocent and that his anger at God is dangerous and misplaced. They argue God is correcting Job, and that he refuses to take God's instruction. They suggest Job doesn't really know or trust God and what God is doing in the world. And today, nothing has really changed. Many of these arguments are still heard from contemporary religious people, and they ring just as false and hurtful to those who are in pain. Job listened to his friends' arguments, but rejected every answer they gave him. Those excuses were much too weak for Job in the face of his profound suffering.

We want our faith to give us all the answers. We want our world to make sense and to know we can trust God to keep us safe, secure, and untroubled, especially if we have devoted ourselves to serving God. But, of course, that's not always the case. Paul wrote his epistles from jail. Most of the disciples died as martyrs. Jesus struggled with God in the garden of Gethsemane. Even he didn't avoid the suffering that was to come. In the Twenty-Third Psalm, God promises to be with us, even when we walk through the valley of the shadow of death, but we don't get to avoid the valleys. As I write this lesson today, the world is in lockdown because of the coronavirus. Everyone is full of fear and uncertainty and is dealing with their own forms of anger, frustration, and bewilderment with God. Like Job, we are dealing with threats to our families, our livelihood, and our health.

There are even some who say the COVID-19 virus is a punishment from God, though that sounds much to me like a response one of Job's friends would give that Job would swiftly reject. While this pandemic has been giving us an opportunity to slow down and take stock of what is important, including our relationship with God, it's hard to believe God would allow the suffering of a worldwide pandemic for those reasons. The simple, frustrating, confounding truth is that we don't know. Our theology is based on human understanding, and therefore it's an imperfect way to try to understand a perfect God. "As James H. Cone in *A Black Theology of Liberation* has put it, 'Sometimes we are better off facing a God whose ways we do not fully understand than working with a theology which claims to provide us with all the answers.'"[1] Job discarded the theology that didn't work to challenge God. The thing we do know is that we don't have to be afraid of confronting God with these difficult questions. God not only allows but welcomes our honesty and vulnerability when we deal with suffering and pain.

1 Taken from *The Vitality of Worship* by Robert Davidson (Grand Rapids, Michigan: William B. Eerdmans Publishing Co., 1998), p. 148.

Maturing in Faith

Job suffered from losing his family, from financial disasters, and then from illness. But his deepest complaints were reserved for those who abandoned him—first his "friends," then other people, and finally God. Losing the support of others was deeply painful to him, yet that often happens when people fall into difficulty. Why do people lose their compassion for others in trouble? What people in our society today, like Job, feel abandoned in their suffering?

Refugees, homeless, the very poor, and the sick come to mind. Sometimes the situation others are in is so foreign to us that it's difficult for us to understand their struggles, and so we don't even try to empathize. When I went to the Mexican-American border recently, I spoke to a young pregnant woman who had walked from Guatemala to the border, hoping to escape the abuses of the drug cartel in her town. I've spoken to homeless

people who have watched others rescue a dog from the streets while ignoring their needs. When I deliver Meals on Wheels, those very short interactions are often the only time the elderly it services sees another human being for weeks. We make excuses. The refugee should work to make a better life in their own country. The homeless should get a job and get off the streets. The elderly must have done something to keep their family or friends away when they needed them. Somehow, it's their fault, and in that case, being compassionate is just being a sucker.

Job's cry was that he didn't do anything to deserve what he got. In today's world, none of us is completely innocent, but all of us are worthy of compassion. Job's cries remind us how important it is to respond to others when they are alone and hurting.

Monday | Psalm 13:1-6
In the midst of fear and tragedy, the psalmist cried out to God for deliverance, yet also sang to God because of God's goodness. God is involved in our lives at every moment, both the tragic and the praiseworthy. We can trust in God's goodness, even in the midst of pain. *Lord, may I trust in your steadfast and ever-present love.*

Tuesday | Job 38:1-14
God controls the shape of the earth and the chaotic seas, setting their limits and forbidding them to go further. Human beings have no power in any of those realms. God's management of creation itself is so vast and incomprehensible that we can't begin to grasp what is involved. *Lord, when I consider your creation, I stand in awe of your great power.*

Wednesday | Job 38:25-38
In a desert society, water is life. God asks Job if he can control the waters and reminds him that rain falls on even the desolate places. God controls the seasons and the stars in the sky, and commands when the rains start each spring. *Oh, God, thank you for the life-giving cycles of seasons that nourish not only your people but all of creation.*

Thursday | Job 40:1-14
Job realizes his mistake in challenging God, but God continues to question him. God asks Job if he believes he has to condemn God in order for him to be innocent (Job 40:8). If Job had the same powers as God, then Job would have the ability to question the structure God created for the world. *Lord, keep me ever mindful of your power and might.*

Friday | Job 41:1-10
It is completely impossible for the Leviathan, the chaos monster, to be controlled by humankind. God's questions to Job show him that the idea that retributive justice (simply following the rules) would hold chaos at bay is a joke. People could no more control chaos in their lives than a child could have the Leviathan as a pet. *Lord, help me to accept all that life may bring me.*

Saturday | Job 42:1-6
Job finally understands his actions do not control his fate. Humbly, he retracts his quest for justice against God and is able to move forward from his tragedies to a life beyond despair. *Lord, help me to understand the role of chaos in creation and learn to live beyond the painful moments in my life.*

Sunday | Job 42:7-17
God blesses Job with double of what he had before. The story ends on an ironic note, but it also reminds us of God's goodness. Job is not rewarded or given restitution, but is blessed by God's grace, a grace which is given room to exist in a world that also accommodates chaos. *Lord, thank you for the existence of both chaos and grace in your creation.*

> **Key Verse:** You said, "Who is this darkening counsel without knowledge?" I have indeed spoken about things I didn't understand, wonders beyond my comprehension. (Job 42:3)

JOB'S RESPONSE TO SUFFERING: ACCEPTANCE

Lesson: Job 40:1-5; 41:1-10; 42:1-6 • **Background:** Job 40:1–42:6; Psalm 13:1-6

Job has asked God for a trial. He feels certain he can defend himself and that God is in the wrong. He has all his questions for God ready and he is sure God will have to capitulate and admit God's guilt. Job believes his relationship with God is based on rewards for righteousness and punishments for sin, and is looking for a black-and-white resolution that names a guilty party. But when God answers, Job soon realizes he is presuming an entirely different worldview and, therefore, asking all the wrong questions. God's answer is to demonstrate that Job's perspective is not the basis of creation at all. God sweeps Job up into a vision of the governance of the entire cosmos. God asks him about the limits of the sea, the placement of the stars, and the care of wild animals. God's initial answer is to challenge Job to try and do all that God is doing. Of course, that is impossible. But it also is a challenge to see creation in the same way as God. The cosmos is not just human beings. It is a swarming mass of living things, knitted together and interacting wildly and wonderfully. It's chaotic but interrelated, all under God's ultimate control. It's beyond even the comprehension of humanity, no less the direction of humanity.

God explains the workings of the cosmos by describing the Behemoth and the Leviathan. The Behemoth and Leviathan are two mythical beasts, perhaps modeled after the hippopotamus and crocodile. The Leviathan and Behemoth are so mighty and ferocious that they are impossible for a human being to tame. They are completely beyond the control of human will because they are both personifications of chaos. They are symbols of the untamed, uncontrolled events, accidents, mysteries, and wonders in the world. In other ancient societies, there were stories about how foreign deities fought the chaos monsters and sought to kill them. However, God explained to Job that God not only allows them to live but cherishes them! In chapters 40 and 41 of Job, God recounts how God created them. Verses 40:15 and 19 tell how the Behemoth was the first of God's acts, created just as God created Job. It is a shockingly different worldview for Job. Rather than fight and try to destroy chaos, God is the source of chaos, and

according to God's account of creation to Job, chaos is an integral part of the cosmos.

This is a completely different understanding of the cosmos than that of the system of reward and punishment that Job had believed in. Job's understanding condemned any form of chaos or anything that didn't follow the rules. According to Job, everyone should get what they deserve, good or bad, and if that didn't happen, then God had failed. He believed he was right to question that failure. Yet, think for a moment what a world like Job originally believed in would actually be like. Everything would be completely predictable. Nothing bad would happen that was undeserved, but on the flip side, nothing good would happen that was undeserved also. There would be no room for mercy. There would be no place for grace. God would be reduced to the role of a cosmic accountant, tallying up pluses and minuses so everyone would get exactly what they deserved. In essence, God would become the servant of human beings, without the freedom to respond in any way except fulfilling what was justified by human actions. Job believed in a manageable God whose actions were based on what Job did. God responds that Job doesn't understand God at all.

A world of untamed chaos would be meaningless. But a world with no possibility for surprise, chance, serendipity, grace, or even evil would be meaningless as well. God's job is not to destroy chaos, but to manage it. God is the only one powerful enough to set boundaries for chaos. God alone can set the limits of the sea (another symbol of chaos) or put a ring in the nose of the mighty Leviathan. When God created the cosmos, God designed a balance that would enable both structure and chaos, both providence and organization. In so doing, God gave humans freedom, but retained freedom as well. God can respond to the events of creation in any way God sees fit, not bound by the rules of reward and punishment.

As human beings, it can be terrifying to understand that chaos is an unescapable part of creation. It means human beings cannot ultimately protect themselves or their loved ones, and that horrible things can happen without any discernible reason. Job's friends clung to the belief that the disasters Job suffered were some sort of moral punishment. As I write this study, I am in lockdown because of the coronavirus, and I have heard many explanations as to why God would punish us with this pandemic. The theology of the Book of Job simply informs us that bad things sometimes happen. It's not necessarily our fault.

When Job replies to God's speech from the whirlwind, he says, "Therefore, I relent and find comfort on dust and ashes" (Job 42:6). This is a key verse that is very difficult to translate. It has many possible meanings and is probably ambiguous on purpose. After all, the entire Book of Job is a statement against black-and-white answers! Other translations say that Job repents or even despises himself. Yet, the CEB translation is one that makes sense to me. The word translated as "relent" (the Hebrew word *ma'ac*) can mean to refuse, reject, melt away, condemn, or withdraw a legal accusation. The Hebrew has no object for the verb, so he probably is not talking about himself. Instead, Job understands his case against God is invalid, and so this translation means simply that he changes his mind about taking God to trial. He doesn't have to protest his innocence. His new understanding of the construct of the world shows him that his suffering isn't due to any guilt or innocence on his part. For this reason, he no longer is bitter or defensive about the tragedies that happened to him. The comfort he found in dust and ashes means he can understand that the human condition is not a result of a capricious, hostile God, but a world where chaos still exists. The cause of his suffering isn't personal, but he does have the love and guidance of the Lord to see him through the ups and downs of an uncertain life. Because Job no longer is obsessed with seeking justice from God, he can leave the dust and ashes behind and begin to heal and move forward with his life.

The Book of Job has a fairy-tale ending to match the "once upon a time" beginning of the story. The book's ironic ending doesn't negate all that came before it, however. Some commentators believe the original story consisted of the first two chapters and the conclusion, and then the middle part was written to struggle with the questions raised by that story. Whatever the conclusion, it does mean that life is not easy to understand and yet again, the world does not follow set and defined rules.

It also reminds us that while God allows chaos to exist in the world, the world is still abundantly filled with God's goodness. Even the wild animals who live in the wastelands are nurtured and loved by God. There is no place that is out of reach of God's presence and care, even the very depths of pain and suffering.

Maturing in Faith

One of the most difficult aspects of the Book of Job is that it asks us to accept mystery as part of our faith. The answer God gives from the whirlwind isn't a thought-out, reasoned answer as to why Job is suffering. God basically says the world is complex and complicated, and that some things just happen, good or bad. As human beings, we can't understand the reasons, if indeed there even are reasons. It's just part of God's design for the world.

God's speech to Job is biting, even sarcastic in places. After all, Job is just a man, challenging the Creator of the universe. My favorite illustration of the huge distance between humanity and God is that Job could no more understand why the world works as it does than my dog could understand algebra. I think it might even be amusing to God that we even try.

That can leave us in an unsatisfying place—a place where we have to accept the mystery and live on faith and trust. But if you read God's answers from the whirlwind again, underneath the demanding questions is a pattern of love and care for the world. God waters all the land, even the desolate places. God knows where the mountain goats have their babies and warms the sand so ostrich eggs hatch. Within this balance of chaos and control, God has constructed a world where creation is sustained and supported. Job felt abandoned and godforsaken, but that was not the reality. Instead, there is no place within creation out of the reach of God's care. There is no condition that can be truly described as godforsaken. We may be troubled—or delighted—by random, chaotic events, but through all of it, we can trust in a God who loves us.

Brain Teaser

All of my flowers except two are **roses**.

All of my flowers except two are **tulips**.

All of my flowers except two are **daisies**.

How many flowers do I have, and what are they?

Three: one rose, one tulip, and one daisy.

Provided by TheTeachersCorner.net

"I'll only give you the paper if you promise not to let the news upset you."

"Hold on, while I connect you to 'Ignore'."

Age is strictly a case of mind over matter. If you don't mind, it doesn't matter.

Jack Benny,
The New York Times (1974)